THIS BOOK BELONGS TO

The Library of

....

....

I can't tell you how grateful I am that you decided to read my book. My most heartfelt thanks that you took time out of your life to choose my work and I hope you find benefit within these pages.

There are so many books available today that offer similar content so that makes it even more humbling that you decided to buying mine.

Tell me what you thought! I am eager to hear your opinion and ideas on what you read as are others who are looking for a good book to buy. Leave a review on Amazon.com so others can benefit from your wisdom!

With much thanks.

TABLE OF CONTENT

SUMMARY

Learning to draw animals can have numerous benefits, both practical and personal. Firstly, it enhances observation skills. When drawing animals, one needs to closely observe their anatomy, proportions, and unique features. This attention to detail trains the eye to notice subtle nuances and improves overall observation skills. This skill can be applied to various aspects of life, such as identifying patterns, analyzing situations, and even enhancing problem-solving abilities.

Secondly, learning to draw animals can improve hand-eye coordination. The process of translating what one sees onto paper requires precise control of hand movements. This coordination between the eyes and hands can be honed through regular practice, leading to improved dexterity and fine motor skills. This can be beneficial in various activities, such as playing musical instruments, participating in sports, or even performing delicate tasks in professions like surgery or art restoration.

Furthermore, drawing animals can be a therapeutic and stress-relieving activity. Engaging in art, including drawing, has been found to reduce stress levels and promote relaxation. The act of focusing on the subject, immersing oneself in the creative process, and expressing emotions through art can provide a sense of calm and tranquility. This can be particularly helpful in today's fast-paced and stressful world, offering a much-needed outlet for self-expression and emotional release.

In addition, learning to draw animals can foster creativity and imagination. Drawing allows individuals to bring their ideas and visions to life, encouraging them to think outside the box and explore their imagination. This can be especially beneficial for children, as it helps develop their cognitive abilities, problem-solving skills, and encourages them to think creatively. Moreover, the ability to visualize and create unique animal characters can be advantageous for individuals pursuing careers in fields such as animation, illustration, or graphic design.

Lastly, learning to draw animals can deepen one's appreciation for nature and wildlife. By closely observing and capturing the beauty of animals through art, individuals develop a greater understanding and connection with the natural world. This can lead to a heightened sense of empathy and environmental consciousness, inspiring individuals to become advocates for animal welfare and conservation.

In conclusion, the benefits of learning to draw animals extend beyond the realm of art. It enhances observation skills, improves hand-eye coordination, provides a therapeutic outlet, fosters creativity and imagination, and deepens appreciation for nature. Whether one aspires to become a professional artist or simply wants to explore a new hobby, learning to draw animals can be a rewarding and enriching experience.

When it comes to nurturing the artistic abilities of young artists, having the right drawing materials is essential. These materials not only allow young artists to express their creativity but also help them develop their skills and techniques. Here are some of the essential drawing materials that every young artist should have:

1. Pencils: A set of high-quality pencils is a must-have for any young artist. Pencils come in different grades, ranging from soft to hard, which allow for various shading and line techniques. It is recommended to have a range of pencils, including HB, 2B, 4B, and 6B, to cater to different drawing styles and subjects.

2. Erasers: Erasers are crucial for correcting mistakes and refining drawings. A kneaded eraser is a versatile option as it can be shaped to erase small details or create highlights. A white vinyl eraser is also handy for erasing larger areas or making precise corrections.

3. Sketchbooks: A good quality sketchbook provides young artists with a dedicated space to practice and experiment. Look for sketchbooks with acid-free paper that can handle different drawing mediums, such as graphite, colored pencils, and markers. The size of the sketchbook depends on personal preference, but a compact and portable option is ideal for young artists on the go.

4. Drawing paper: Apart from sketchbooks, having a stack of loose drawing paper is essential for young artists. Drawing paper comes in various weights and textures, such as smooth or rough. It is recommended to have a variety of paper options to explore different drawing techniques and mediums.

5. Colored pencils: Colored pencils are a fantastic medium for young artists to add vibrant colors to their drawings. Look for a set of colored pencils that offer a wide range of colors and are easy to blend. Watercolor pencils are also a great option as they can be used dry or with water to create beautiful washes and gradients.

6. Markers: Markers are another versatile drawing tool that young artists can use to add bold lines and vibrant colors to their artwork. Look for markers that are non-toxic and have a fine tip for precise details. Water-based markers are a safer option for young artists as they are easier to wash off skin and clothing.

7. Charcoal: Charcoal is a unique drawing medium that allows young artists to create bold and expressive drawings.

Drawing a squirrel can be a fun and rewarding activity. Whether you are an experienced artist or just starting out, following a step-by-step guide can help you create a realistic and detailed squirrel drawing. Here is a more detailed explanation on how to draw a squirrel:

1. Gather your materials: Start by gathering all the necessary materials for your drawing. You will need a pencil, eraser, paper, and any coloring tools you prefer, such as colored pencils or markers.

2. Observe squirrel anatomy: Before you start drawing, take a moment to observe the anatomy of a squirrel. Notice the shape of its body, the position of its limbs, and the proportions of its head and tail. This will help you create a more accurate representation of a squirrel in your drawing.

3. Start with basic shapes: Begin your drawing by lightly sketching the basic shapes that make up the squirrel's body. Start with an oval shape for the head, a larger oval for the body, and smaller ovals for the limbs. Use light, loose lines to create these shapes, as they will serve as your guidelines.

4. Add details to the face: Once you have the basic shapes in place, start adding details to the squirrel's face. Sketch the eyes, nose, and mouth, paying attention to their placement and proportions. Squirrels have large, round eyes, a small nose, and a mouth that is often hidden by their fur.

5. Define the body: After you have the face sketched out, start defining the squirrel's body. Add more curves and contours to the body shape, making it appear more three-dimensional. Pay attention to the position of the limbs and the shape of the tail, as these are important features of a squirrel.

6. Refine the details: Once you have the basic structure of the squirrel in place, it's time to add more details. Start by adding fur texture to the body, using short, curved lines to create a sense of depth and realism. Pay attention to the direction of the fur, as it tends to follow the contours of the body.

7. Add shading and highlights: To make your squirrel drawing more realistic, add shading and highlights. Observe the light source in your reference image or imagine where the light is coming from. Use darker shading to create depth and lighter highlights to add dimension to the drawing.

Drawing a monkey can be a fun and creative activity. Here is a step-by-step guide on how to draw a monkey in a more detailed and longer format:

1. Start by drawing a large oval shape for the monkey's head. Make sure to leave some space at the bottom for the body.

2. Next, draw two small circles on the upper part of the oval shape to represent the monkey's ears.

3. Now, draw two large circles for the monkey's eyes. Place them towards the center of the head, leaving some space in between. Add small circles inside the eyes to represent the pupils.

4. Below the eyes, draw a curved line for the monkey's nose. Add two small curved lines on each side of the nose to create the nostrils.

5. Moving on to the mouth, draw a curved line below the nose. Add a small curved line at the end of the mouth to create a smile.

6. To create the monkey's face, draw a curved line from the top of the head, curving down towards the sides of the oval shape. This will form the outline of the monkey's face.

7. Now, let's draw the monkey's body. Start by drawing two curved lines extending from the bottom of the head, curving towards each other. Connect these lines at the bottom to create the monkey's torso.

8. Draw two curved lines extending from the torso to create the monkey's arms. Add small ovals at the end of each line to represent the hands.

9. Moving on to the legs, draw two curved lines extending from the bottom of the torso. Curve these lines slightly outward to create the monkey's thighs. Add two more curved lines below the thighs to create the lower legs.

10. To complete the legs, draw small ovals at the end of each line to represent the monkey's feet.

11. Now, let's add some details to the monkey's face. Draw a curved line above each eye to represent the monkey's eyebrows. Add a small curved line below each eye to create the cheekbones.

12. Next, draw a curved line from the top of the head to the back of the body to create the monkey's back.

13. To add some texture to the monkey's body, draw small curved lines all over the torso, arms, and legs. This will give the appearance of fur.

14. Finally, erase any unnecessary lines and add some color to your monkey drawing.

Drawing a dolphin can be a fun and creative activity that allows you to showcase your artistic skills. Whether you are a beginner or an experienced artist, following a step-by-step guide can help you achieve a realistic and visually appealing dolphin drawing. Here's a detailed explanation on how to draw a dolphin:

1. Start by sketching the basic shape of the dolphin's body. Begin with a curved line that resembles an elongated oval. This will serve as the dolphin's torso.

2. Next, draw a slightly curved line extending from the front of the torso to create the dolphin's snout. Make sure the line is tapered and pointed at the end.

3. To add the dolphin's mouth, draw a small curve that connects the snout to the torso. This curve should be slightly open to depict the dolphin's smiling expression.

4. Now, it's time to draw the dolphin's eye. Place a small oval shape near the top of the snout, slightly to the side. Add a smaller circle within the oval to represent the pupil. Leave a small white space to create a highlight, giving the eye a realistic look.

5. Moving on to the dolphin's fins, draw a curved line starting from the top of the torso, extending towards the back. Repeat this step on the other side to create the dorsal fin. For the pectoral fins, draw two curved lines on each side of the torso, slightly below the head.

6. To complete the dolphin's body, draw a curved line starting from the bottom of the torso, extending towards the back. This will form the tail. Add a few curved lines within the tail to represent the flukes.

7. Now, it's time to add some details to make your dolphin drawing more realistic. Start by adding a curved line along the dolphin's back to create the dorsal ridge. Add a few curved lines on the torso to represent the dolphin's skin texture.

8. To give your dolphin a sense of movement, draw a few curved lines around the fins and tail, indicating the flow of water.

9. Once you are satisfied with the overall shape and details of your dolphin, it's time to add some color. Dolphins are commonly known for their grayish-blue color, but you can use your creativity and choose any color you like. Consider adding shades and highlights to make your drawing more vibrant and three-dimensional.

Drawing a hummingbird can be a fun and rewarding experience. These small, vibrant birds are known for their quick movements and beautiful colors, making them a popular subject for artists. If you're interested in learning how to draw a hummingbird, here are some steps to help you get started.

1. Gather your materials: Before you begin, make sure you have all the necessary materials. You will need a pencil, eraser, paper, and colored pencils or markers if you want to add color to your drawing.

2. Start with basic shapes: Begin by lightly sketching the basic shapes that make up the hummingbird's body. Start with an oval shape for the body and a smaller oval or circle for the head. Add a long, curved line for the beak and two small circles for the eyes.

3. Add details: Once you have the basic shapes in place, start adding more details to your drawing. Use reference images or observe real

hummingbirds to help you accurately depict their features. Add feathers to the body, making sure to show the texture and patterns. Pay attention to the wings, which are usually long and narrow, and the tail, which is often fan-shaped.

4. Refine the outline: Once you're satisfied with the overall shape and details, go over your sketch with a darker pencil or pen to create a more defined outline. Use smooth, flowing lines to capture the graceful nature of the hummingbird.

5. Add color: If you want to add color to your drawing, now is the time to do so. Hummingbirds come in a variety of colors, so feel free to get creative with your color choices. Use colored pencils or markers to carefully fill in the feathers, making sure to blend the colors smoothly for a realistic effect.

6. Shade and highlight: To add depth and dimension to your drawing, use shading and highlighting techniques. Observe how light falls on the hummingbird's body and feathers, and use your pencil or marker to create areas of shadow and areas of light. This will make your drawing appear more three-dimensional.

7. Final touches: Once you're happy with your drawing, take a step back and assess it. Are there any areas that need further refinement or adjustment? Use your eraser to make any necessary corrections. You can also add additional details, such as flowers or a background, to enhance your drawing further.

Drawing a horse can be a fun and rewarding activity for both beginners and experienced artists. Whether you want to create a realistic representation or a more stylized version, there are a few key steps to keep in mind.

First, start by sketching the basic shapes that make up the horse's body. Begin with a large oval for the main body, and then add a smaller circle on one end for the head. Connect these shapes with a curved line to form the neck. Next, draw a long, slightly curved line extending from the body to create the back. From the back, add another curved line to form the hindquarters and tail.

Once you have the basic shapes in place, you can start adding more details. Begin by refining the head shape, adding the ears, eyes, and nostrils. Pay attention to the proportions and placement of these features to ensure a realistic look. The eyes should be almond-shaped and placed slightly forward on the head, while the ears should be pointed and positioned on top of the head.

Moving on to the body, add the legs by drawing long, slender lines extending from the appropriate places on the body. Horses have long, elegant legs, so be sure to capture their graceful shape. Pay attention to the angles and proportions of the legs to maintain a sense of realism. Add hooves at the bottom of each leg, making sure they are proportionate to the size of the horse.

Next, focus on the details of the horse's face and body. Add a mane along the neck, using flowing lines to create a sense of movement. Horses also have a distinct muscular structure, so consider adding some definition to the body by lightly sketching in the muscles. Pay attention to the contours of the body and the way the muscles connect to create a sense of depth and realism.

Once you are satisfied with the overall shape and details of the horse, you can move on to adding shading and texture. This step is optional, but it can greatly enhance the realism of your drawing. Use light and dark shading to create depth and dimension, paying attention to the direction of light source to create realistic highlights and shadows. Consider using cross-hatching or stippling techniques to add texture to the horse's coat.

Finally, don't forget to erase any unnecessary guidelines and refine your drawing. Take your time to add any final touches and make any necessary adjustments.

To draw a Stegosaurus, follow these step-by-step instructions:

1. Start by drawing the basic shape of the Stegosaurus's body. Begin with a large oval shape for the body, slightly elongated horizontally. This will serve as the main framework for the dinosaur.

2. Next, draw a smaller oval shape towards the rear of the body, which will represent the Stegosaurus's hip area. Connect this oval to the main body using curved lines.

3. Now, it's time to add the head. Draw a small oval shape at the front of the body, slightly overlapping the main body oval. Connect the head to the body using a curved line.

4. Once the head is in place, draw the Stegosaurus's neck. Start from the back of the head and draw a long, curved line that connects to the body. Make sure to give the neck a slight curve to add a more realistic touch.

5. Moving on to the tail, draw a long, curved line extending from the rear of the body. The tail should be thick at the base and gradually taper towards the end. Add small triangular spikes along the top of the tail, starting from the base and getting smaller towards the tip.

6. Now, let's focus on the legs. Draw four short, thick lines extending from the bottom of the body. These will serve as the Stegosaurus's legs. Add small, rounded shapes at the end of each leg to represent the feet.

7. To give the Stegosaurus its iconic appearance, draw a row of large, diamond-shaped plates along its back. Start from the base of the neck and continue all the way to the tail. These plates should be evenly spaced and gradually decrease in size towards the tail.

8. Finally, add the details to the face. Draw a small, rounded eye on the side of the head, followed by a small nostril on the tip of the snout.

9. Once you have finished drawing the basic outline, go over your lines with a darker pencil or pen to make them more defined. Erase any unnecessary guidelines or overlapping lines.

10. Now it's time to bring your Stegosaurus to life with color! Stegosauruses are often depicted with earthy tones, such as shades of green, brown, and gray.

Drawing a unicorn can be a fun and creative activity that allows you to bring your imagination to life. Whether you are an experienced artist or just starting out, here are some steps to help you draw a unicorn in a more detailed and realistic manner.

1. Start by sketching the basic shape of the unicorn's head. Draw a large oval shape for the head and add a smaller oval shape for the snout. Connect these two shapes with a curved line to create the unicorn's face.

2. Next, draw the unicorn's ears. These can be long and pointed, similar to a horse's ears. Place them on top of the head, slightly angled outward.

3. Now, it's time to draw the unicorn's horn. Position it in the center of the head, between the ears. The horn can be curved or straight, depending on your preference. Make it pointy and slightly twisted to give it a magical appearance.

4. Moving on to the eyes, draw two large oval shapes on either side of the snout. Add smaller circles inside the ovals to represent the pupils. You can also add some eyelashes to make the eyes more expressive.

5. To create the unicorn's mane, draw a series of curved lines starting from the top of the head and flowing down the neck. These lines can be

wavy and uneven to give the mane a more natural look. You can also add some extra details like strands of hair or braids to make it more interesting.

6. Now, let's draw the unicorn's body. Start by sketching a long, curved line that extends from the bottom of the head to create the back. Then, draw another curved line that connects to the back and forms the belly. Add a smaller curved line to create the hind leg.

7. Moving on to the front legs, draw two more curved lines that extend from the bottom of the head and connect to the belly. These lines should be slightly shorter than the hind leg. Add hooves at the end of each leg by drawing small oval shapes.

8. To complete the unicorn's body, draw a long, curved line that connects the hind leg to the front leg. This line represents the unicorn's back leg. Add a hoof at the end of this leg as well.

9. Finally, add some details to your unicorn drawing. You can draw a tail by sketching a long, flowing line that extends from the back of the unicorn's body.

When it comes to coloring and adding details to drawings, there are several tips and techniques that can help enhance your artwork and make it more visually appealing. Whether you are working with traditional mediums like colored pencils or markers, or digital tools like graphic tablets and software, these tips can be applied to various mediums.

Firstly, it is important to choose the right colors for your drawing. Consider the mood and atmosphere you want to convey and select a color palette that complements it. You can use color theory principles such as complementary colors (colors opposite each other on the color wheel) to create contrast and make certain elements stand out. Additionally, experimenting with different shades and tones of a color can add depth and dimension to your artwork.

When it comes to coloring, it is crucial to have a consistent and even application of color. This can be achieved by using light, controlled strokes and building up layers gradually. Start with lighter colors as a base and gradually add darker shades to create shadows and highlights. Blending colors together using techniques like shading or cross-hatching can also create smooth transitions and gradients.

Adding details to your drawing can bring it to life and make it more visually interesting. Pay attention to small elements like textures, patterns, and intricate designs. These details can be added using various techniques such as stippling (creating patterns using small dots), hatching (creating patterns using parallel lines), or even using different tools like brushes or pens with different tips.

Another important aspect of adding details is paying attention to proportions and perspective. Ensure that the details you add are in proportion to the overall composition and that they follow the correct perspective. This will make your drawing look more realistic and cohesive.

Furthermore, consider the use of different mediums and techniques to add texture and depth to your artwork. For example, you can experiment with different types of paper or surfaces to create interesting textures. You can also use techniques like layering, glazing, or dry brushing to add depth and dimension to your drawings.

Lastly, practice and experimentation are key to improving your coloring and detailing skills. Don't be afraid to try new techniques, explore different styles, and learn from other artists. Take inspiration from nature, photographs, or even other artworks to develop your own unique style.

In conclusion, coloring and adding details to drawings require careful consideration of color choices, consistent application, attention to detail, and understanding of proportions and perspective. By following these tips and techniques, you can enhance your artwork and create visually stunning drawings.

The journey of becoming a skilled young artist is a transformative and challenging process that requires dedication, passion, and a strong work ethic. It is a path that is filled with both triumphs and setbacks, but ultimately leads to personal growth and artistic development.

At the beginning of this journey, a young artist may have a natural talent or inclination towards art, but they often lack the technical skills and knowledge needed to create truly exceptional work. They may start by experimenting with different mediums and styles, exploring their own creativity and finding their unique artistic voice. This stage is crucial as it allows the artist to discover their strengths and interests, and lays the foundation for their future growth.

As the young artist progresses, they begin to seek out formal education and training. This could involve enrolling in art classes, attending workshops, or even pursuing a degree in fine arts. These educational experiences provide the artist with the opportunity to learn from experienced professionals, gain a deeper understanding of art history and theory, and develop their technical skills. They may study various techniques such as drawing, painting, sculpture, or digital art, and learn how to effectively use different tools and materials.

However, education alone is not enough to become a skilled young artist. Practice and perseverance are essential components of the journey. The artist must dedicate countless hours to honing their craft, pushing themselves to experiment, take risks, and constantly improve. They may spend hours in the studio, working on their pieces, refining their skills, and pushing the boundaries of their creativity. This process can be frustrating and demanding, but it is through this dedication that the artist begins to see significant progress and growth.

Along the way, the young artist may face numerous challenges and setbacks. They may experience self-doubt, criticism, or rejection from others. However, these obstacles serve as opportunities for the artist to develop resilience and determination. They learn to embrace failure as a stepping stone towards success, and to use criticism as a tool for improvement. Each setback becomes a valuable lesson that helps them refine their artistic vision and strengthen their resolve.

As the young artist continues on their journey, they may also seek out opportunities to showcase their work and gain recognition. This could involve participating in art exhibitions, entering competitions, or even starting their own online portfolio. These experiences not only provide exposure for the artist, but also allow them to receive feedback from a wider audience and connect with other artists and art enthusiasts.

HOW TO DRAW

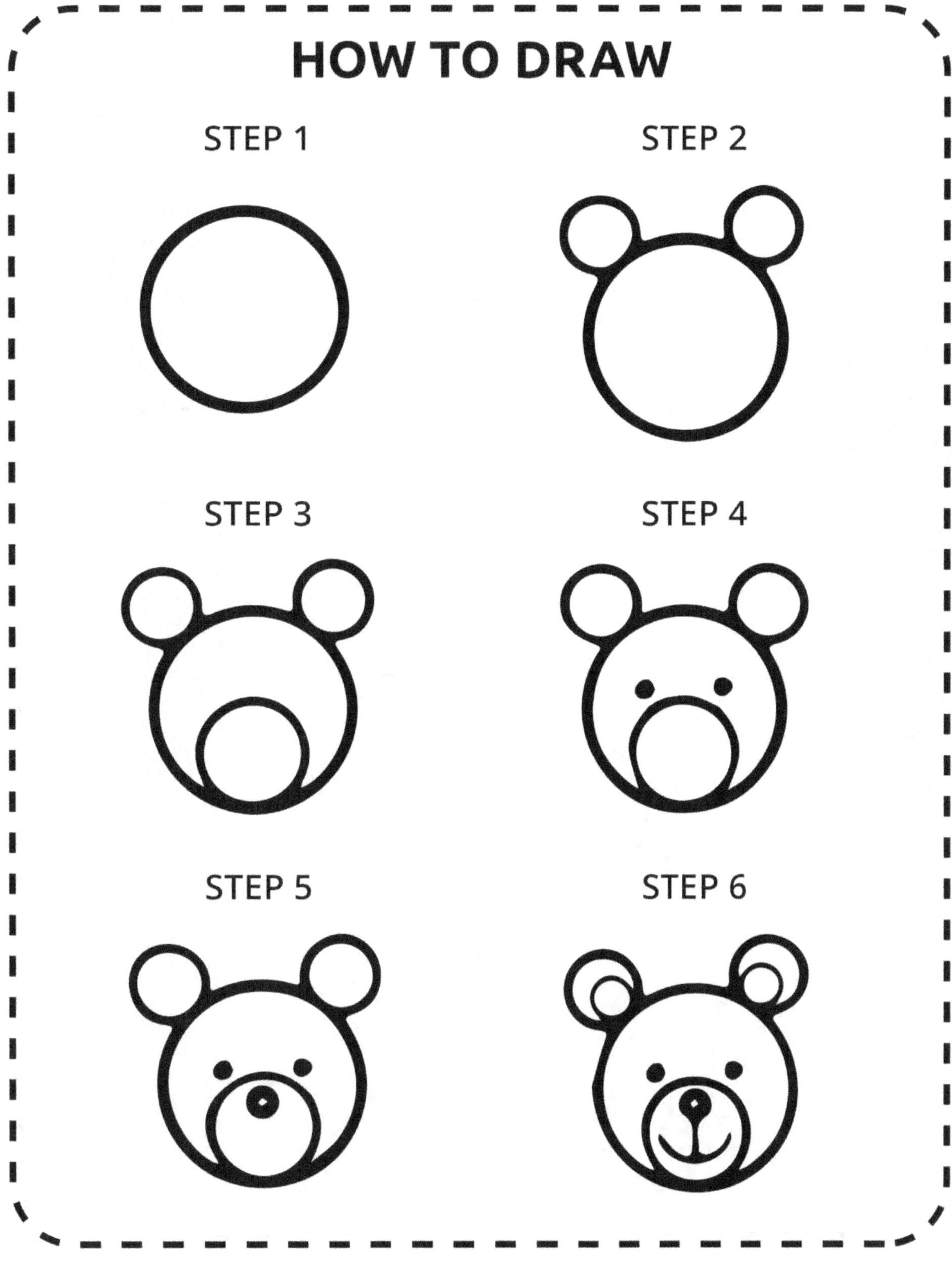

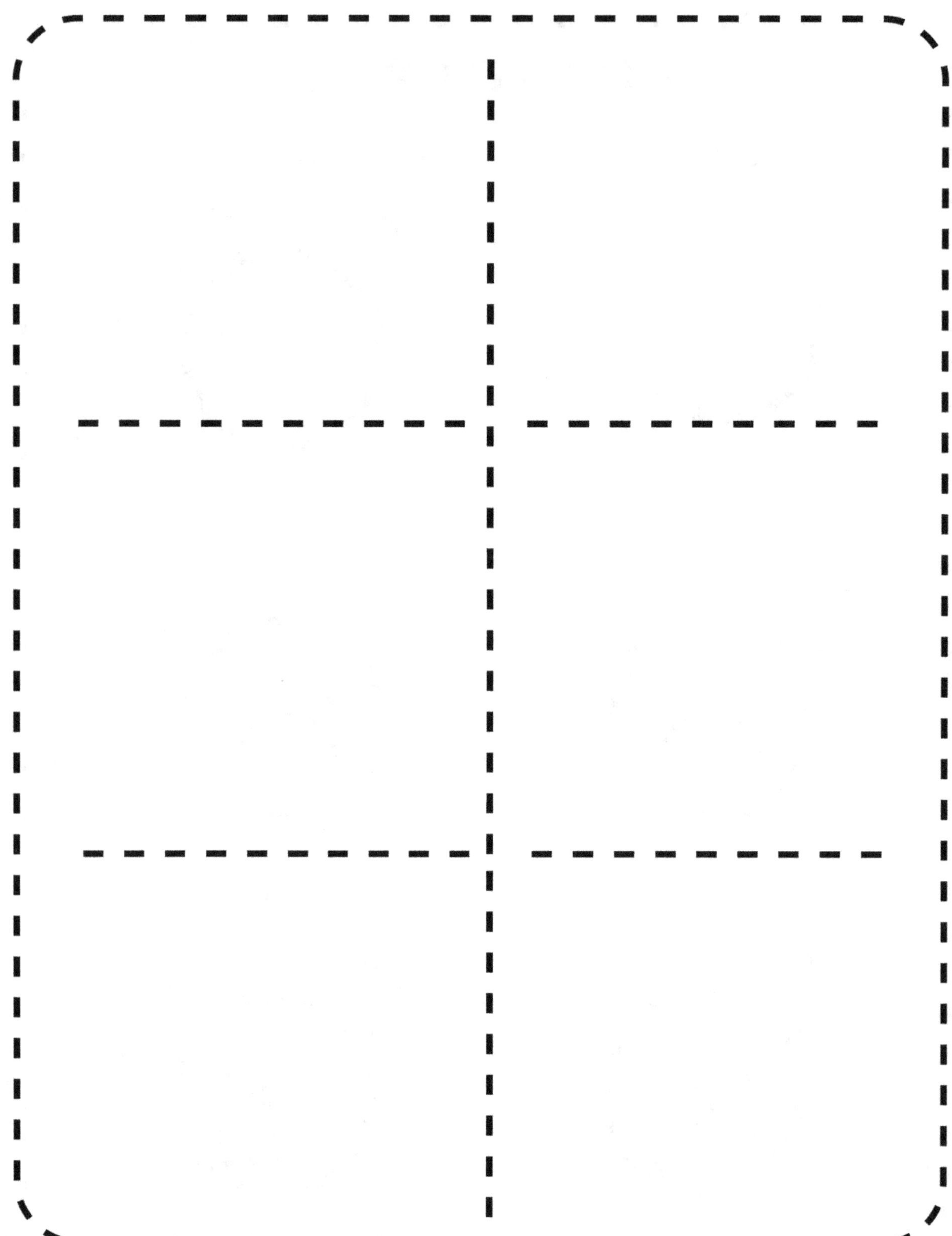

HOW TO DRAW

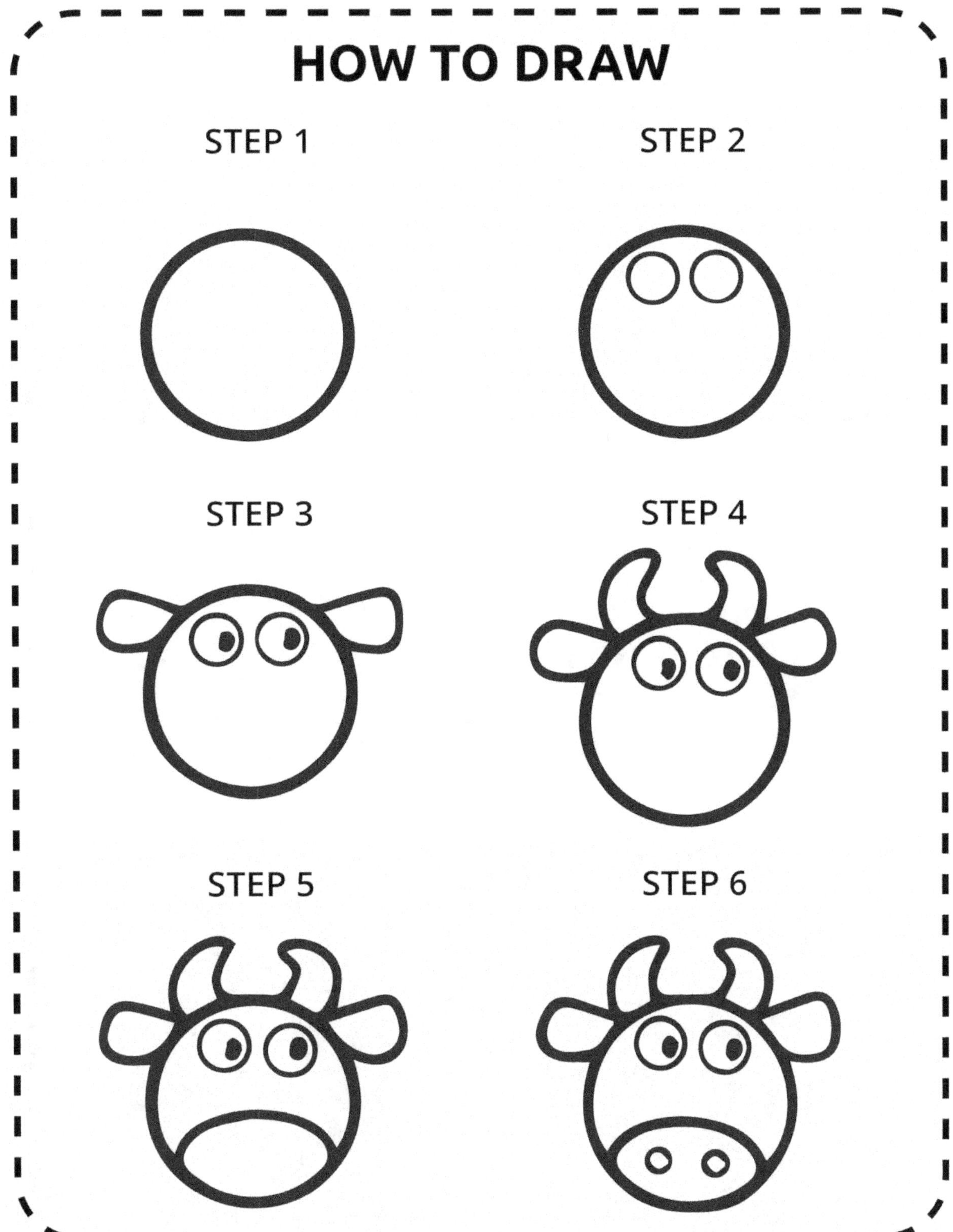

HOW TO DRAW

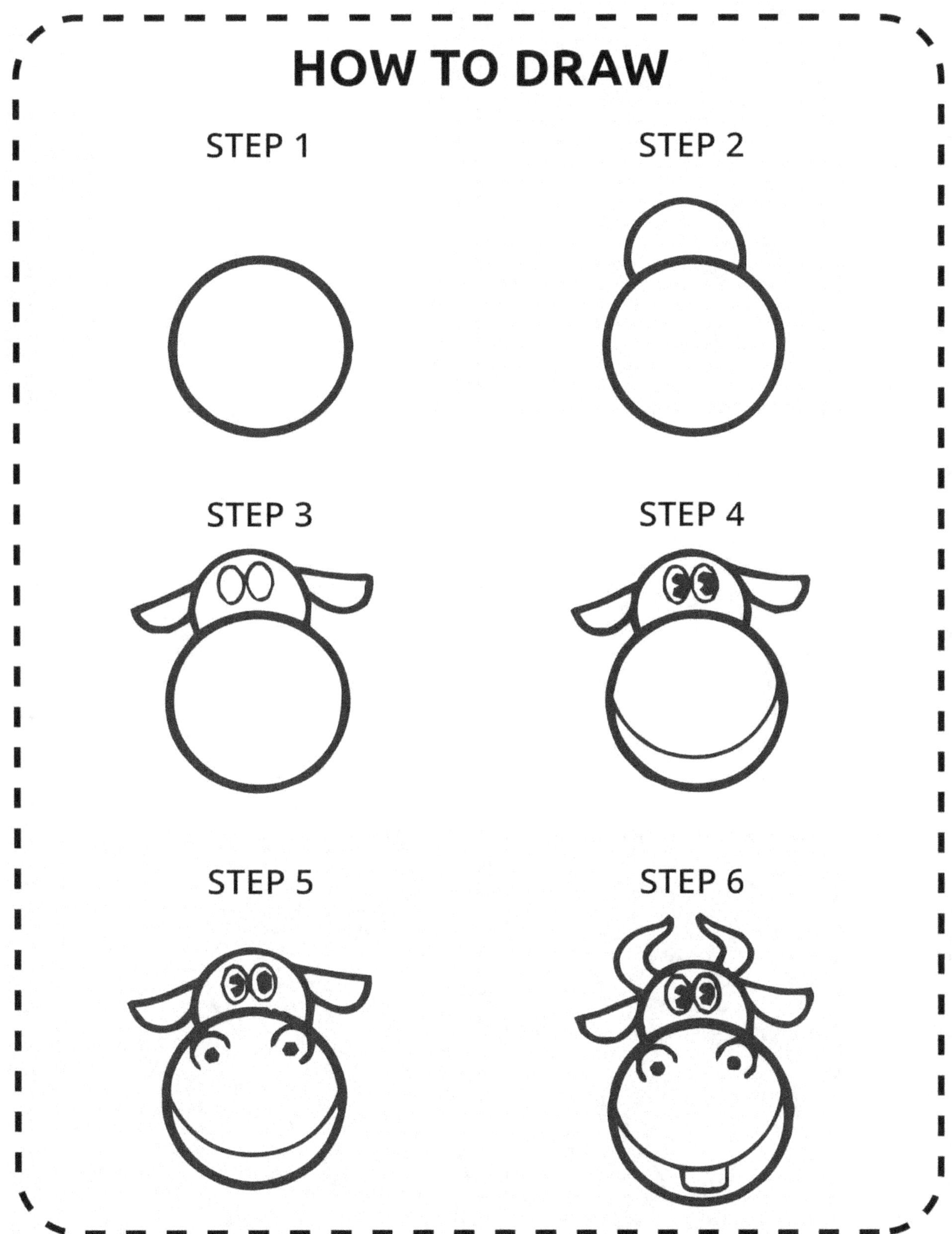

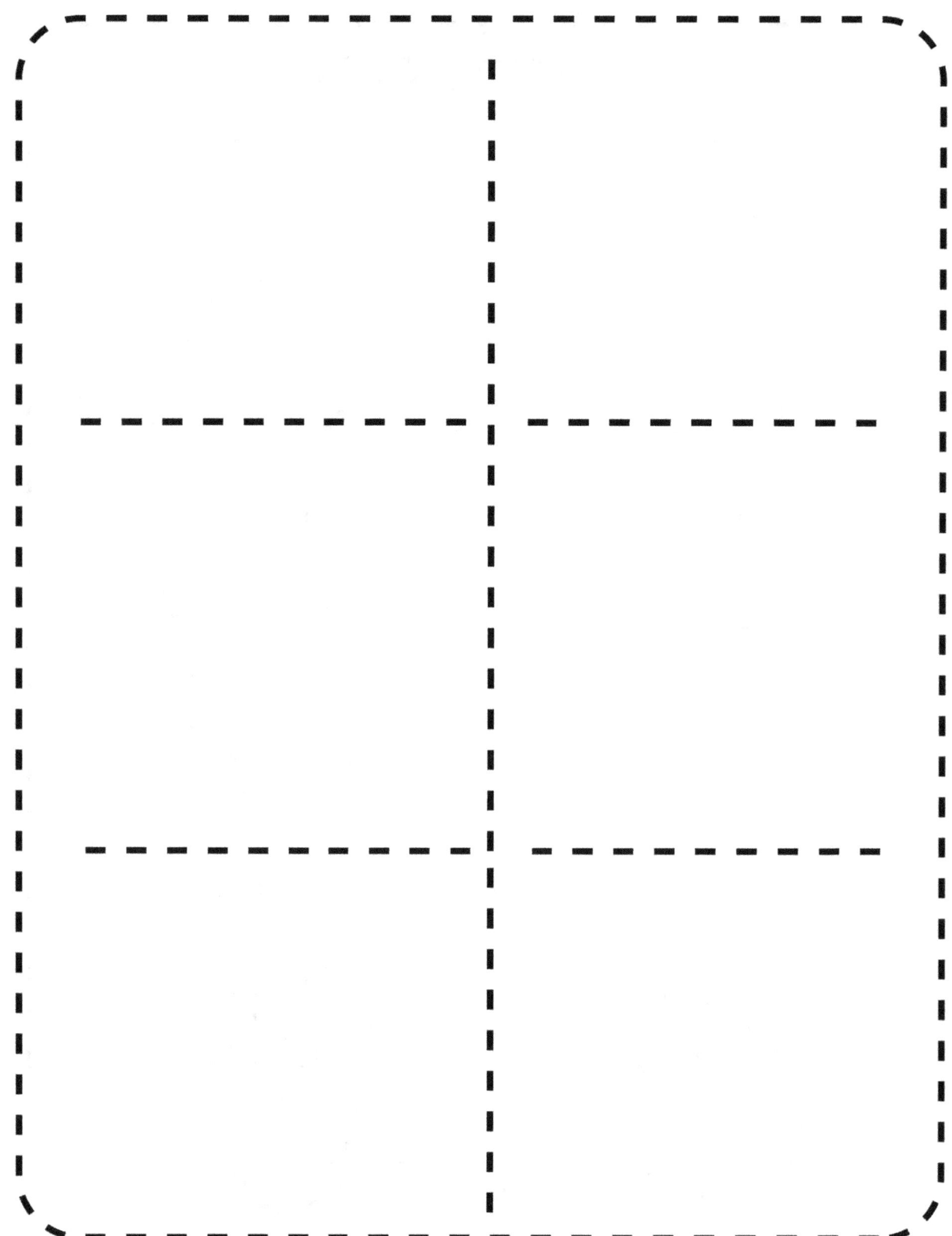

HOW TO DRAW

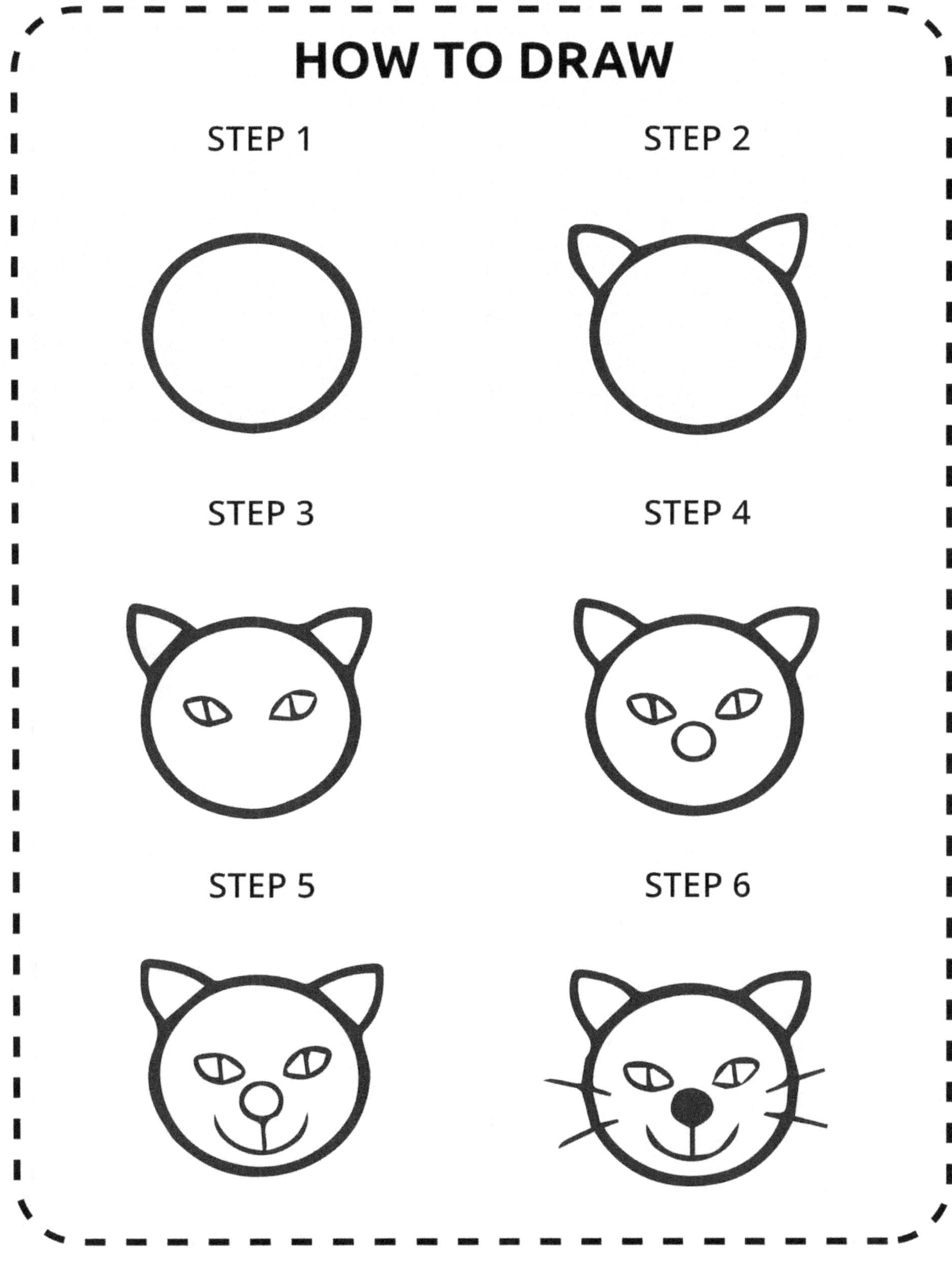

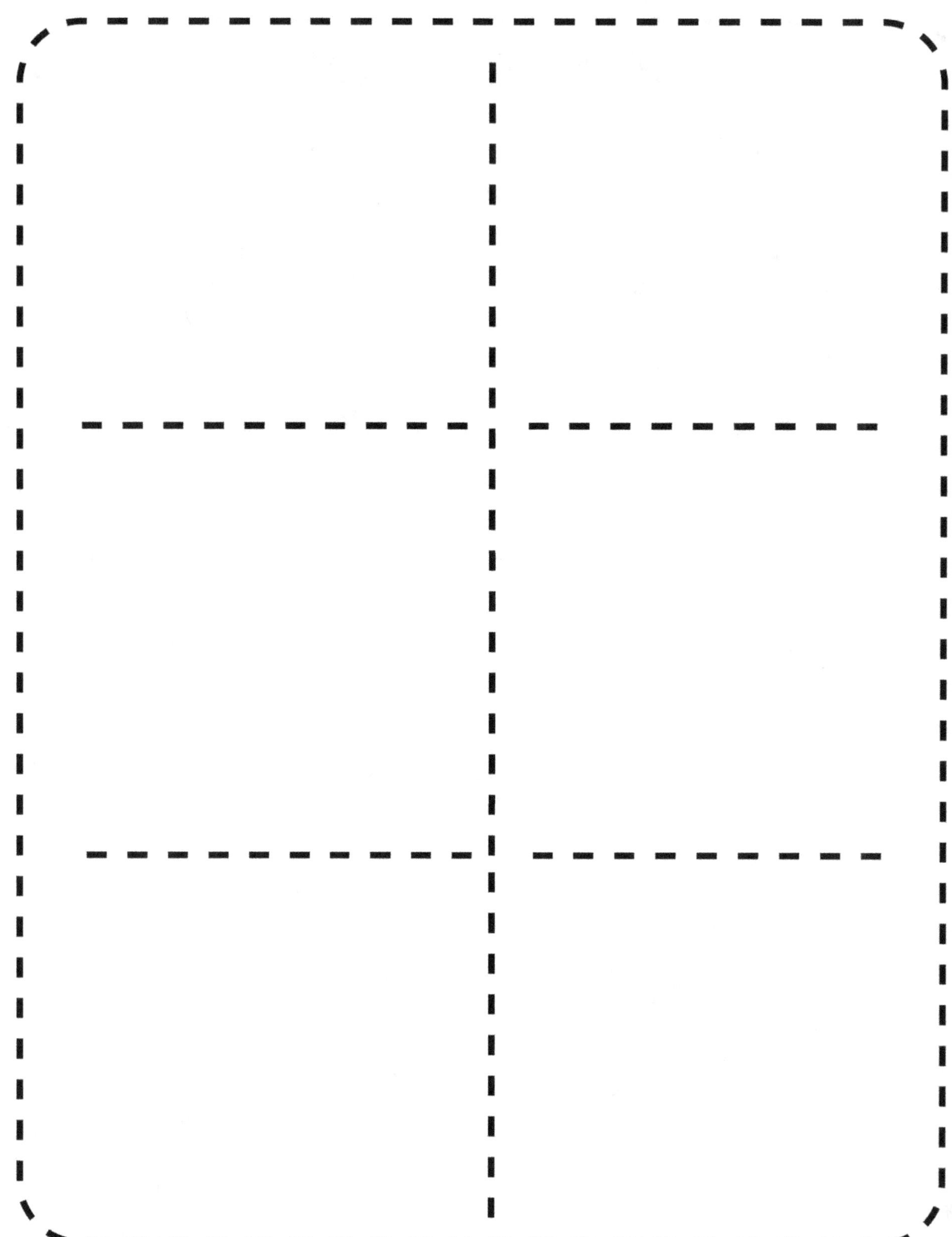

HOW TO DRAW

STEP 1

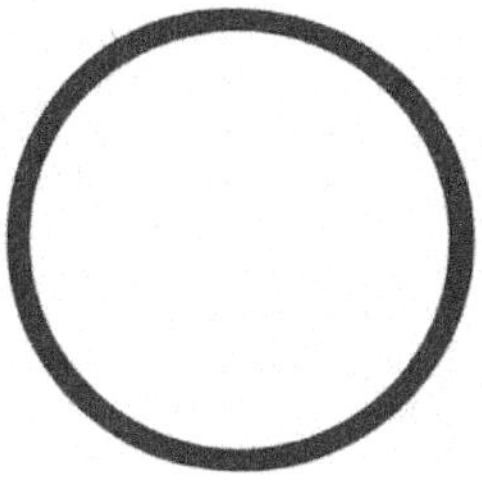

STEP 2

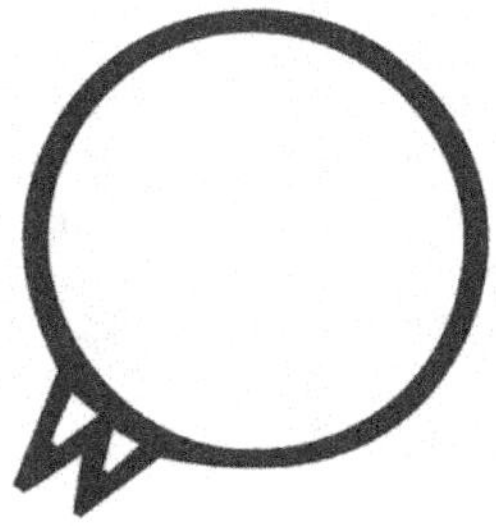

STEP 3

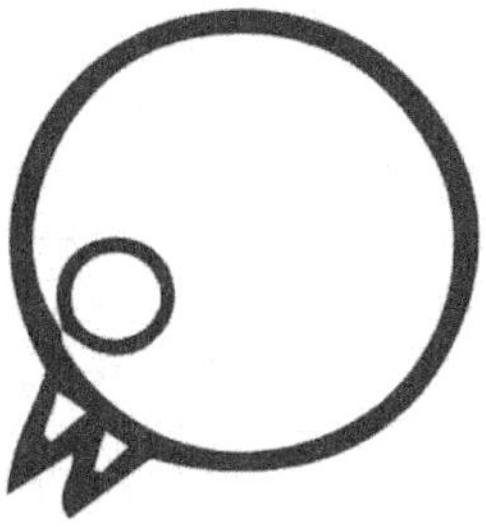

STEP 4

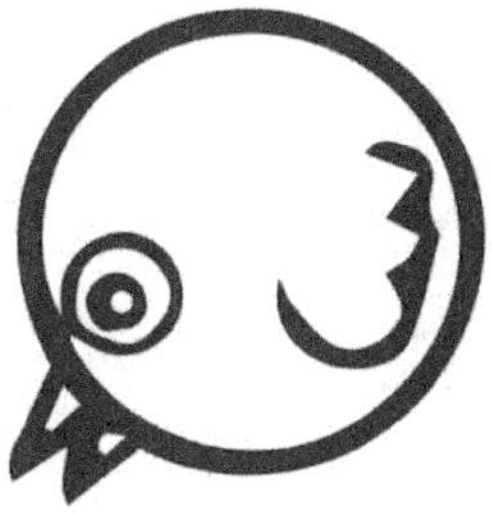

STEP 5

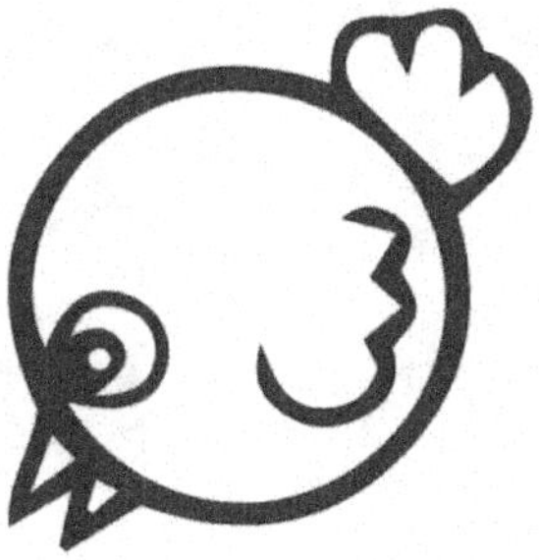

STEP 6

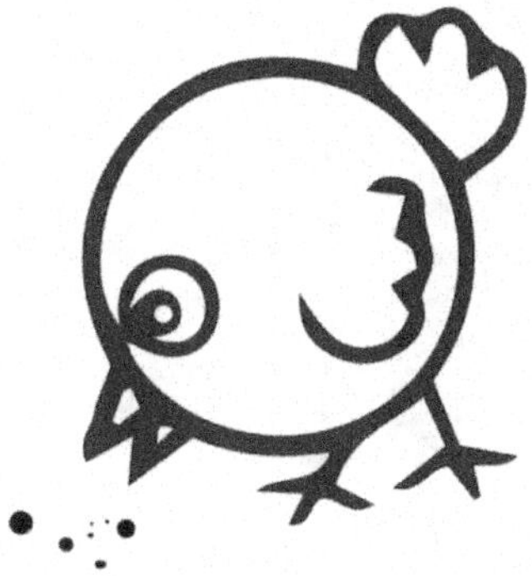

HOW TO DRAW

STEP 1

STEP 2

STEP 3

STEP 4

STEP 5

STEP 6

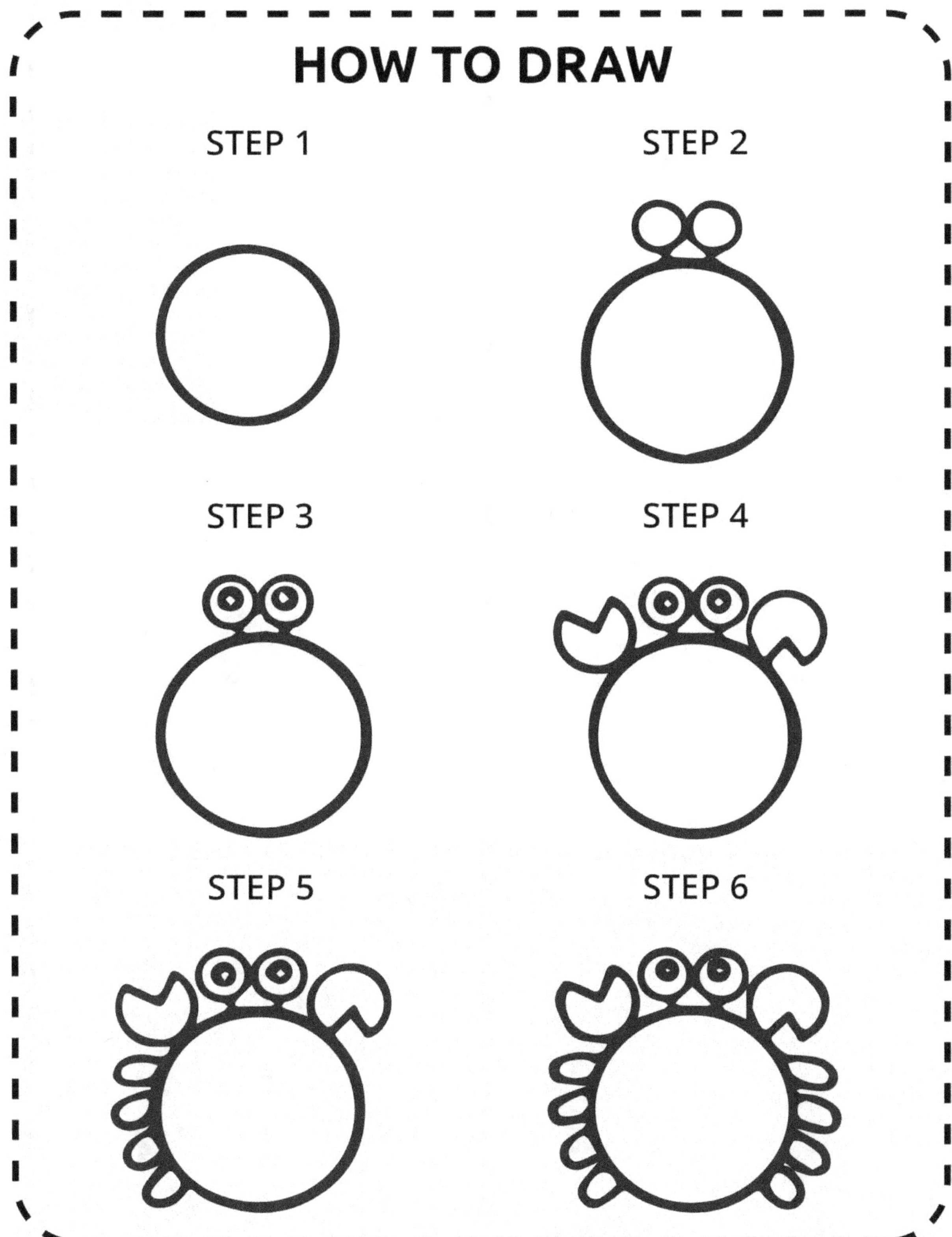

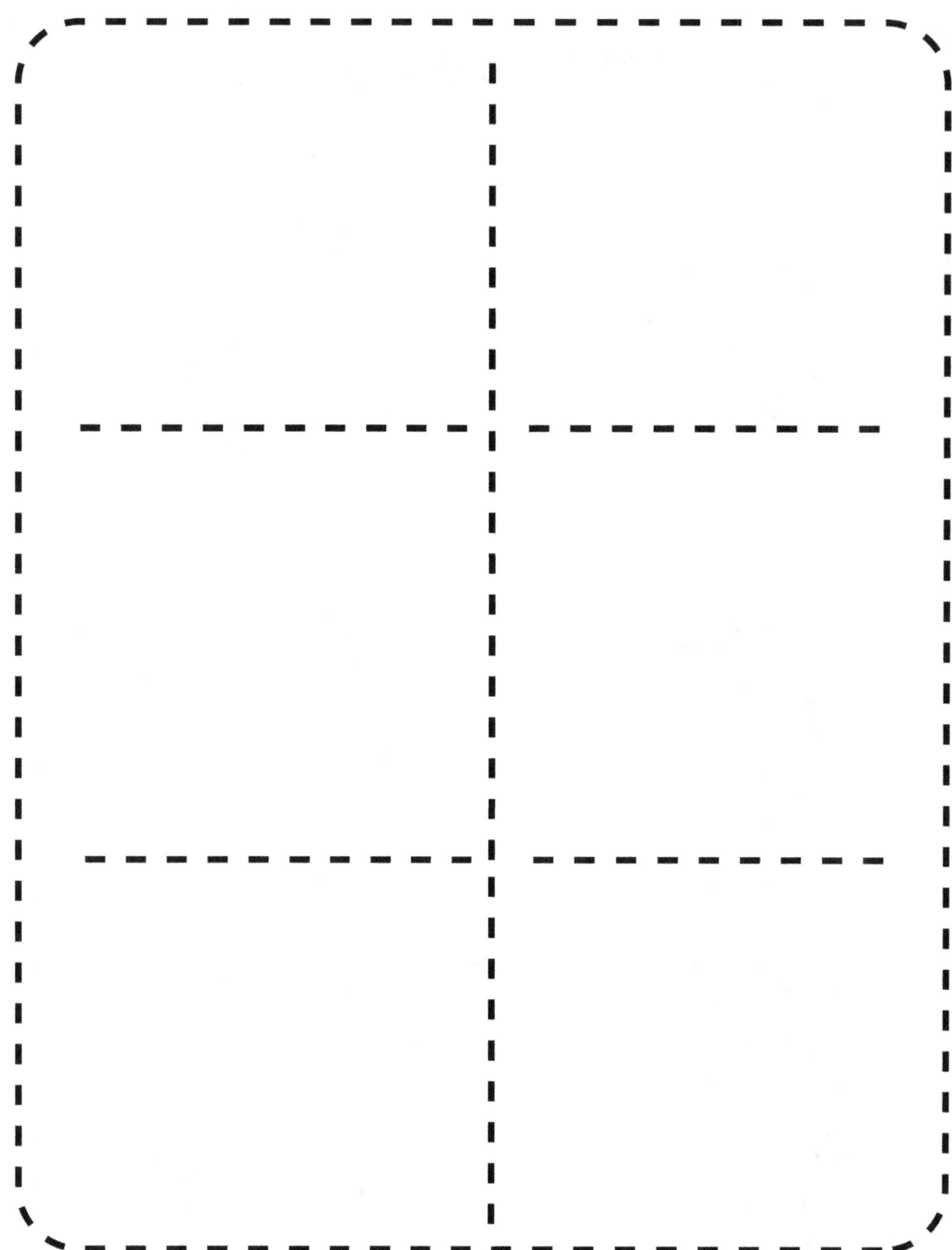

HOW TO DRAW

STEP 1

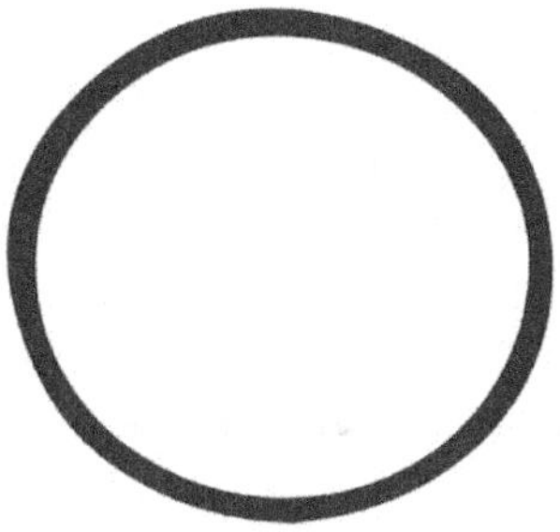

STEP 2

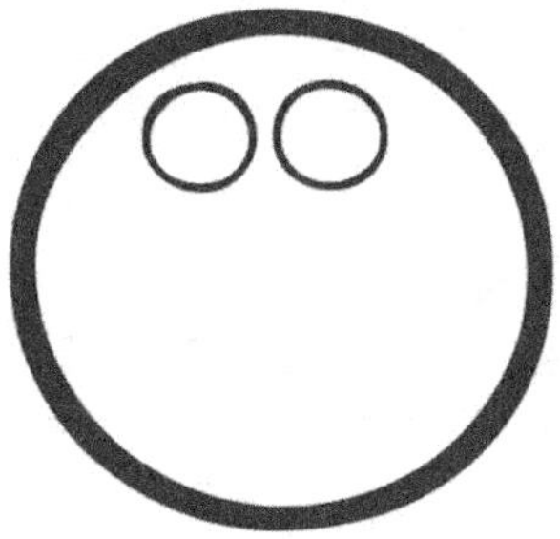

STEP 3

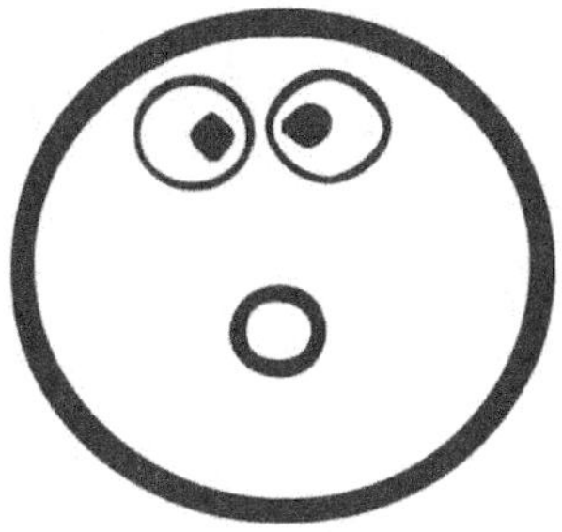

STEP 4

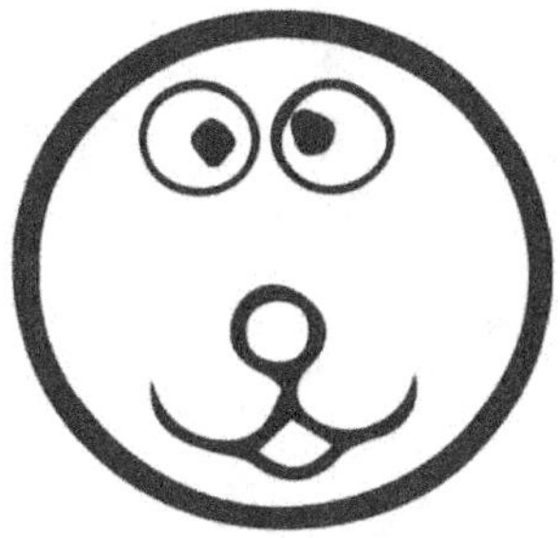

STEP 5

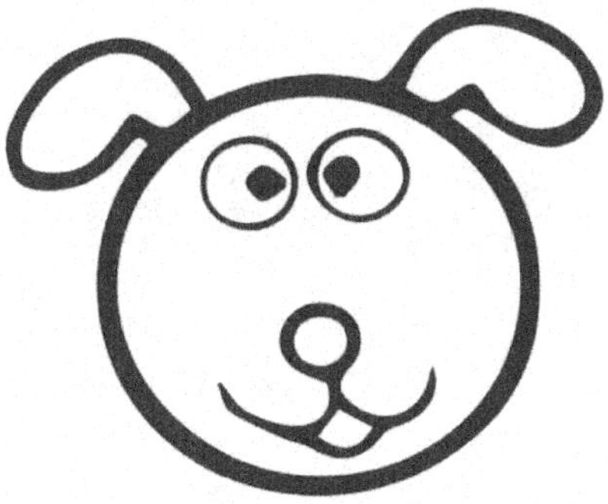

STEP 6

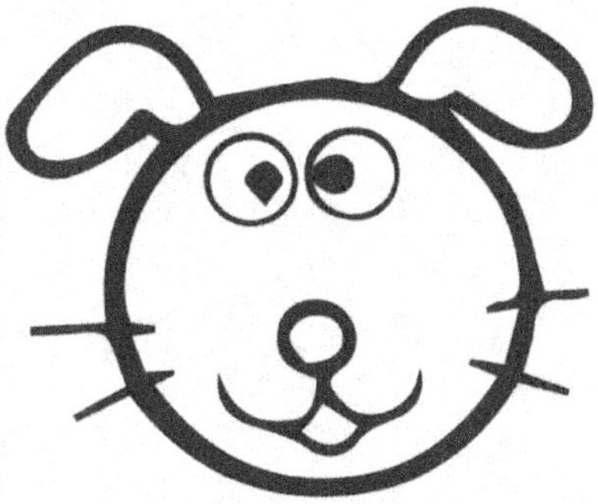

HOW TO DRAW

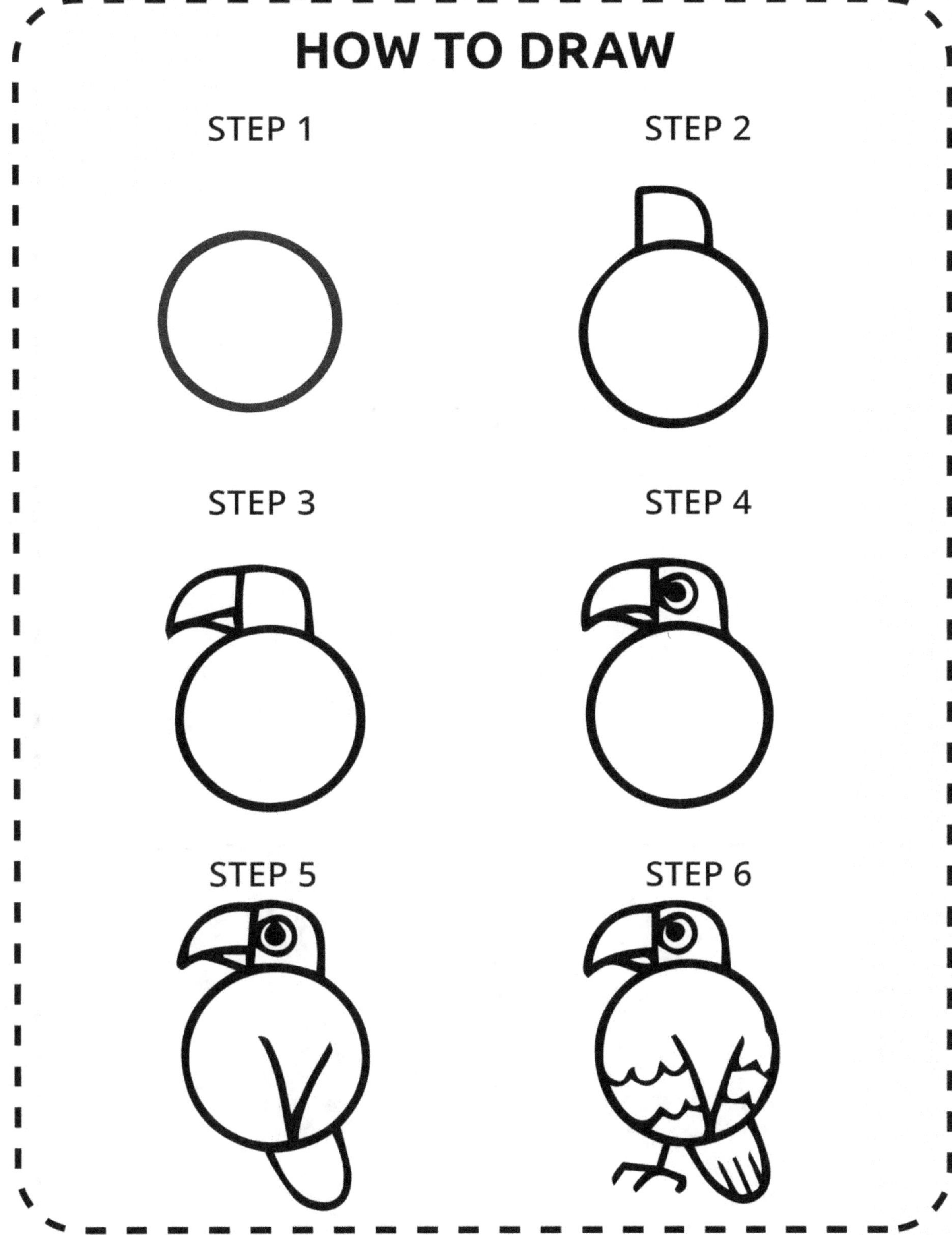

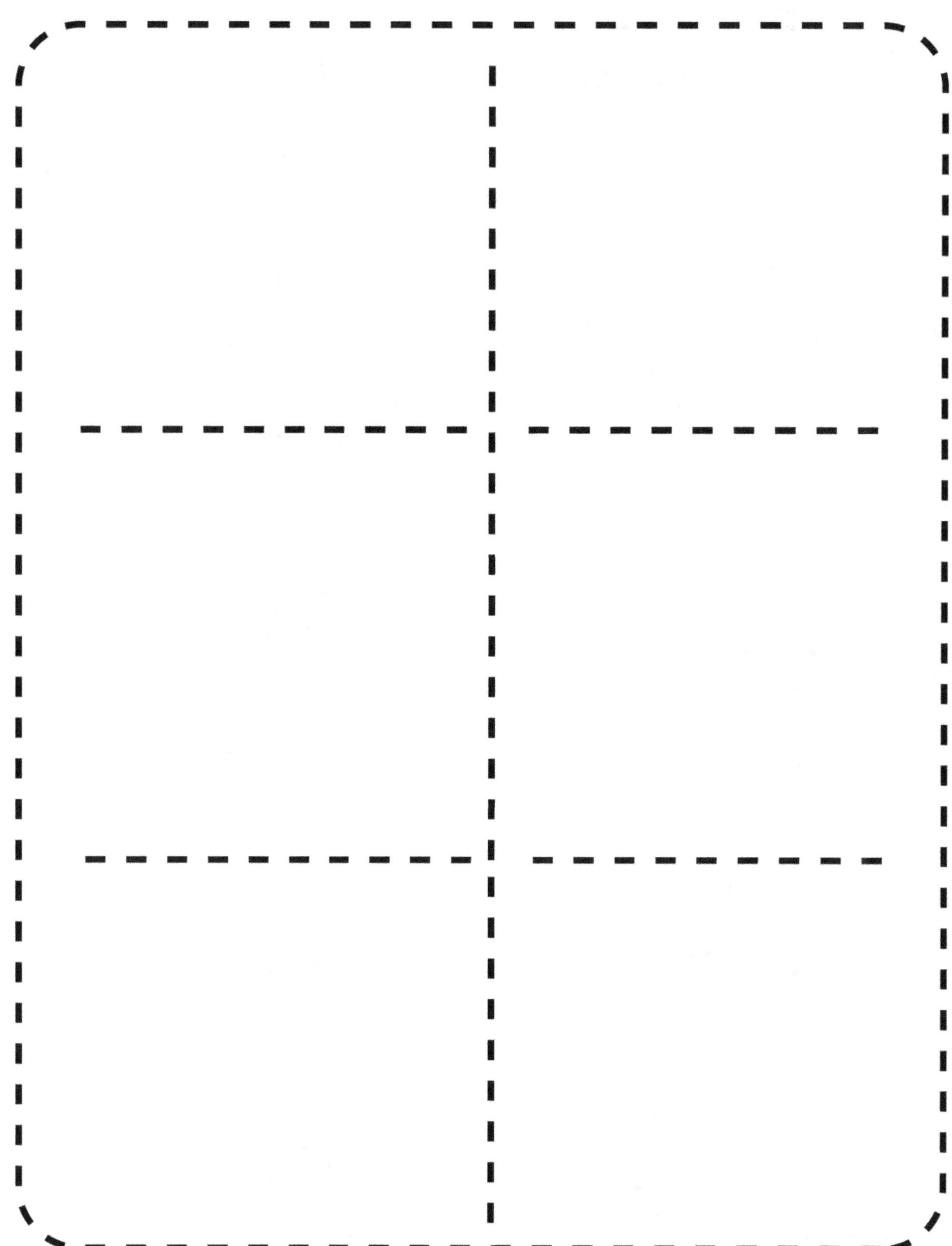

HOW TO DRAW

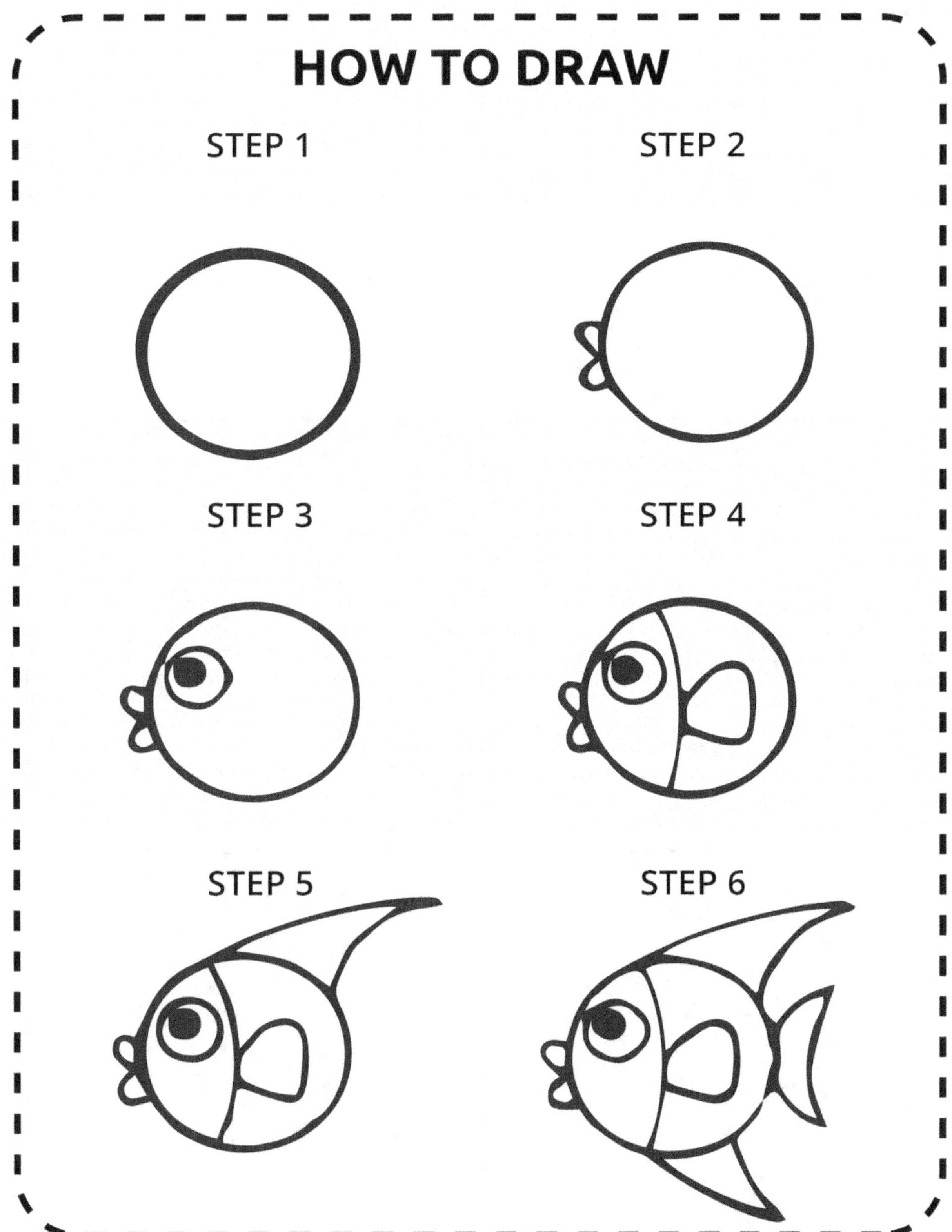

HOW TO DRAW

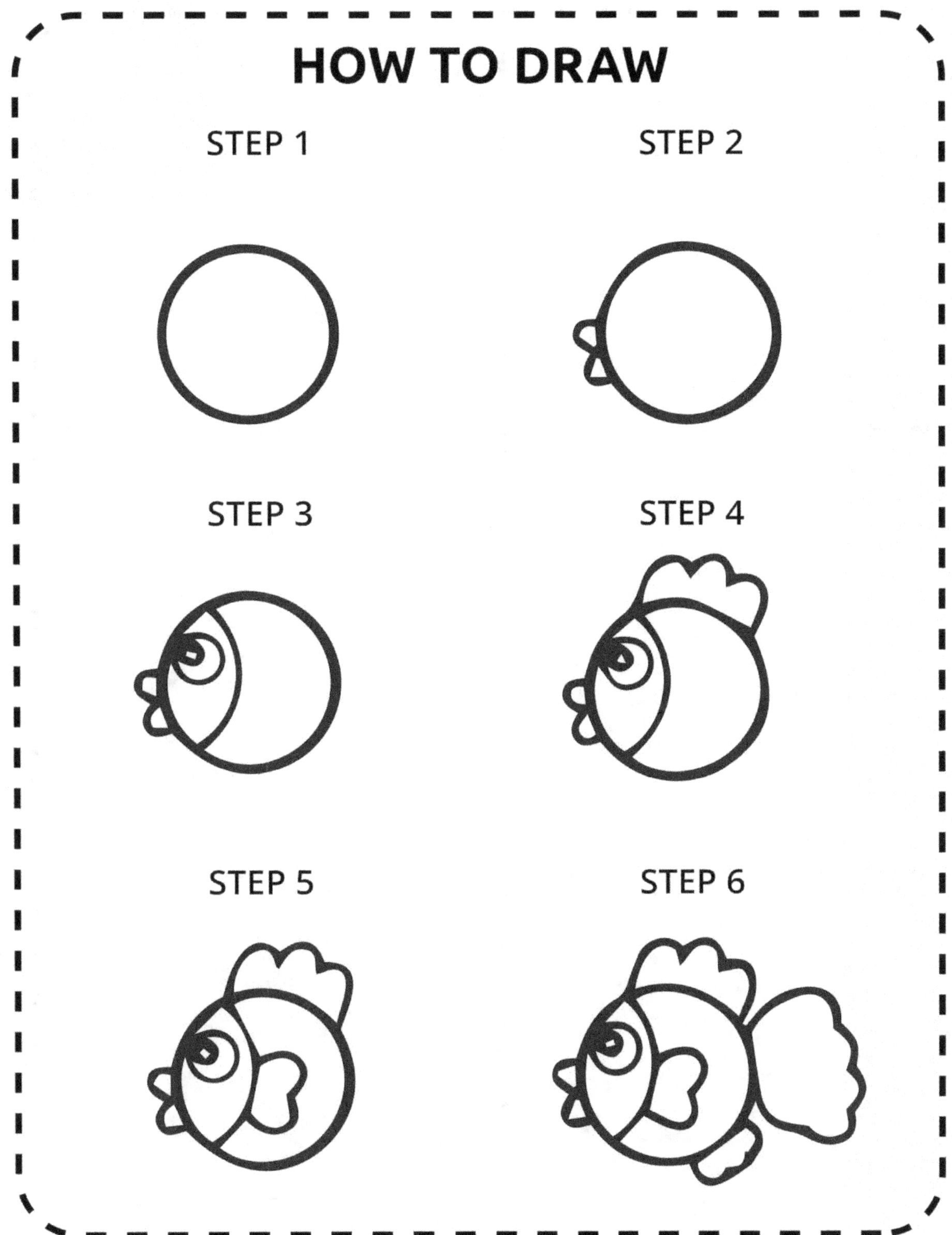

HOW TO DRAW

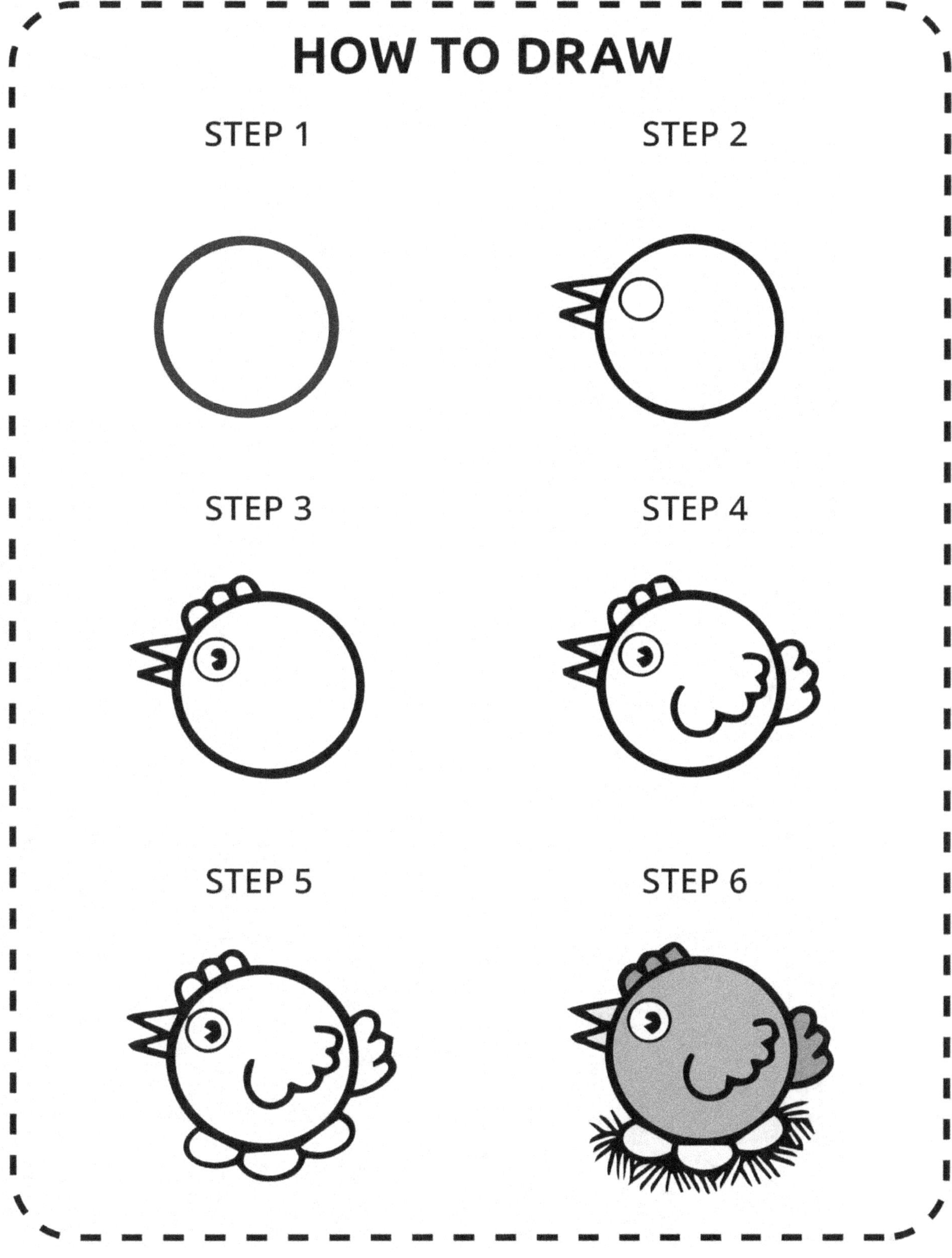

HOW TO DRAW

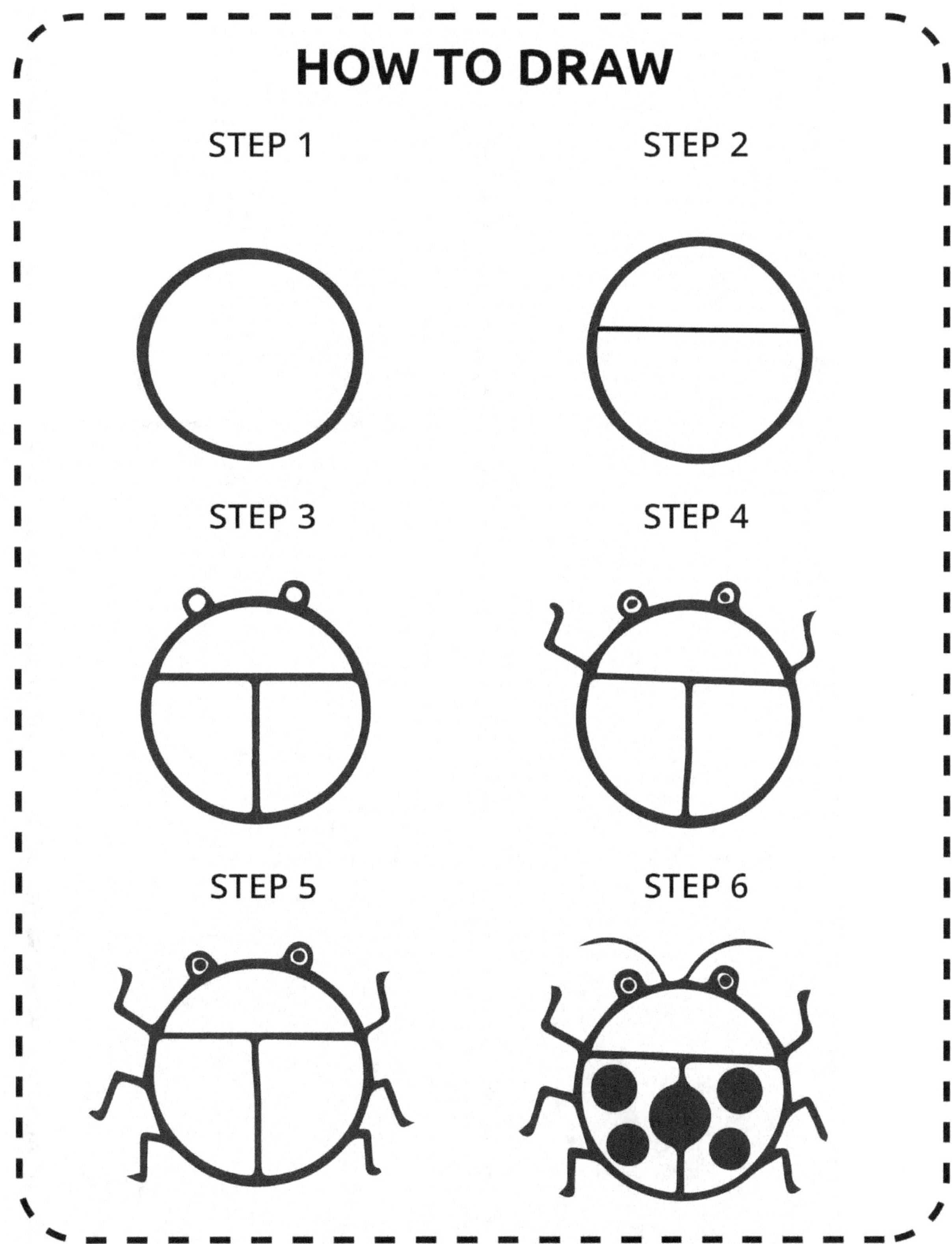

HOW TO DRAW

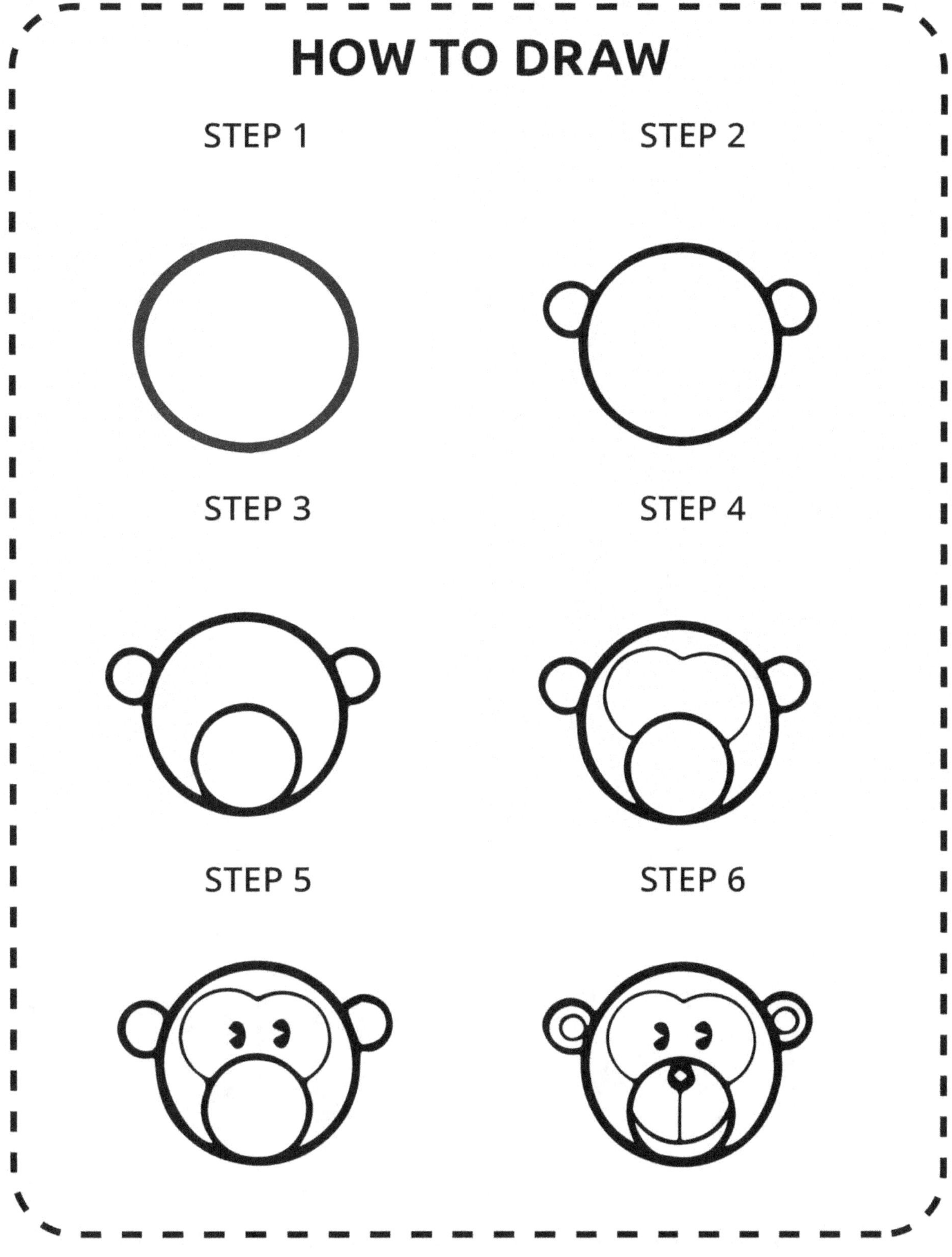

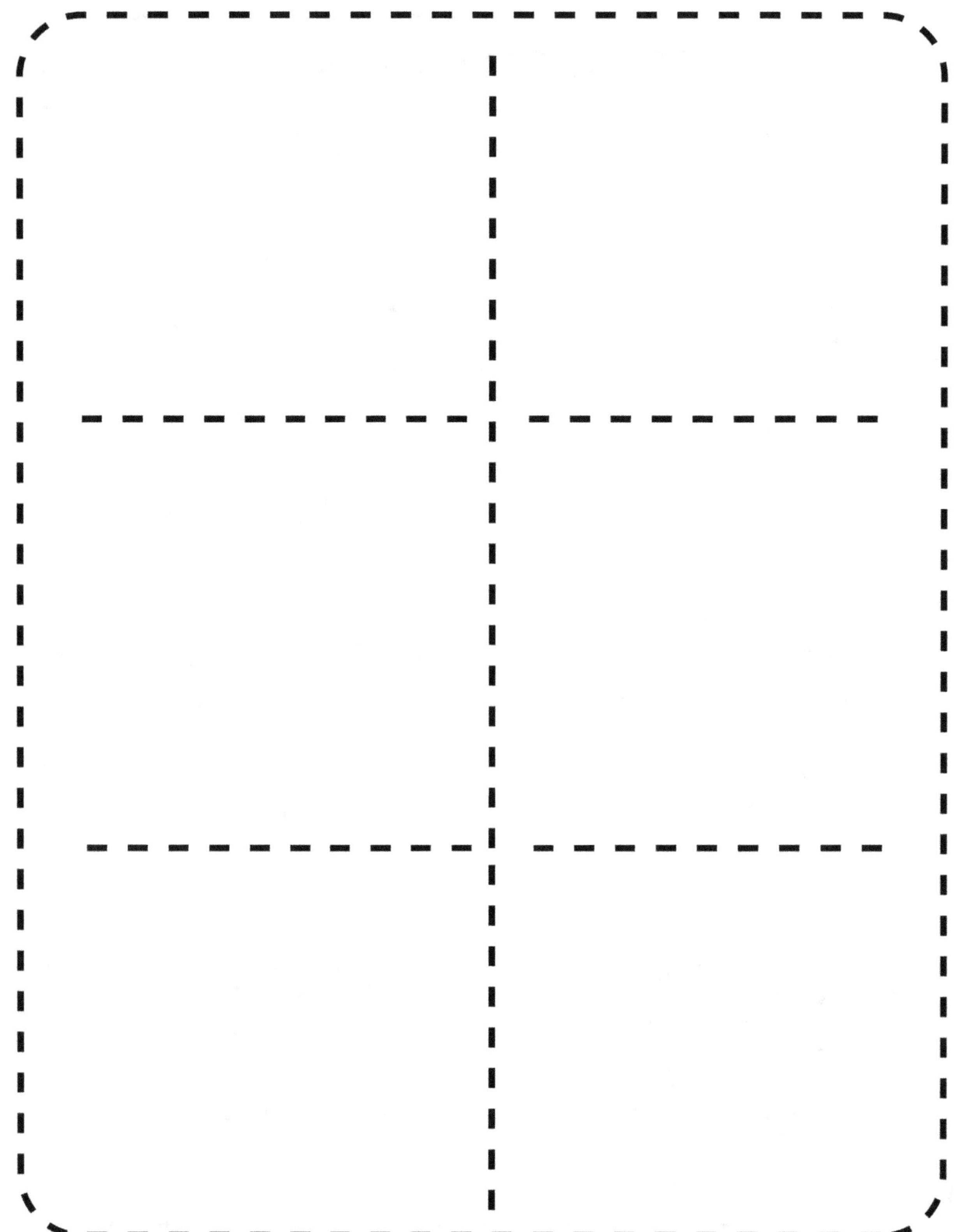

HOW TO DRAW

STEP 1

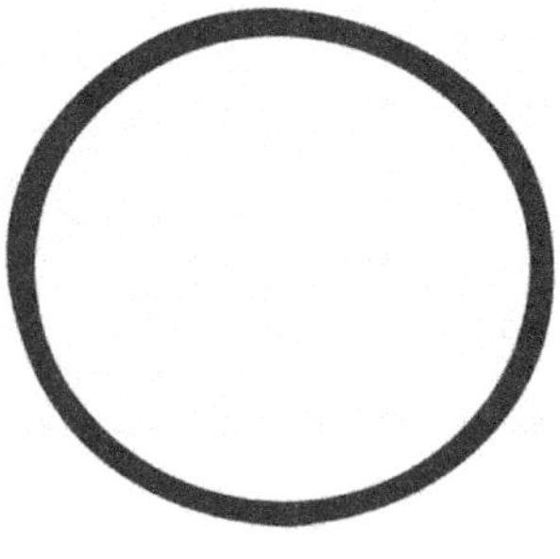

STEP 2

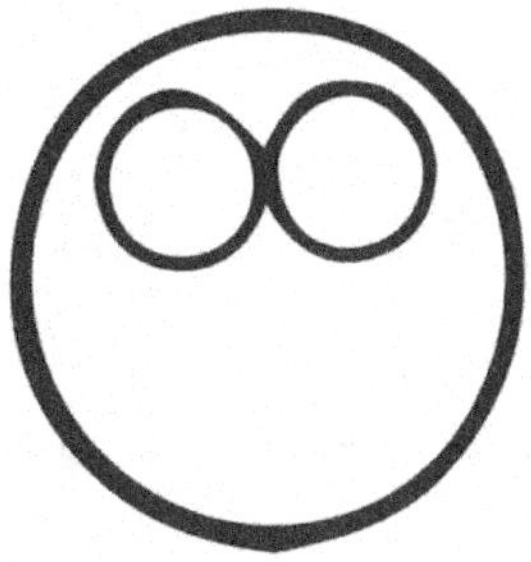

STEP 3

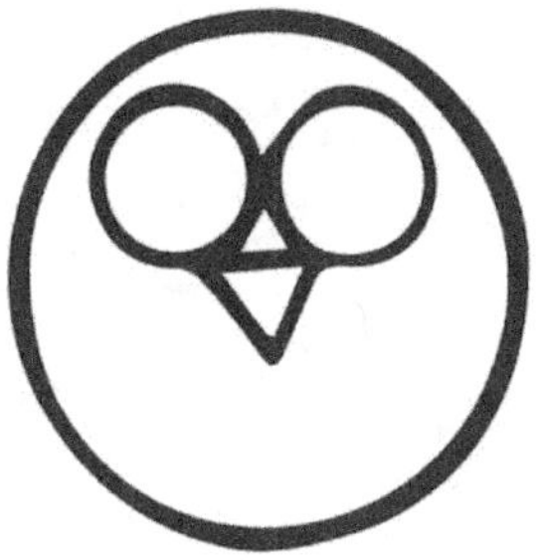

STEP 4

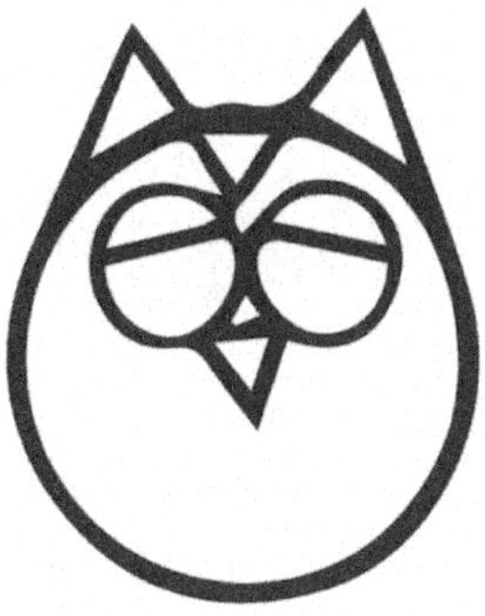

STEP 5

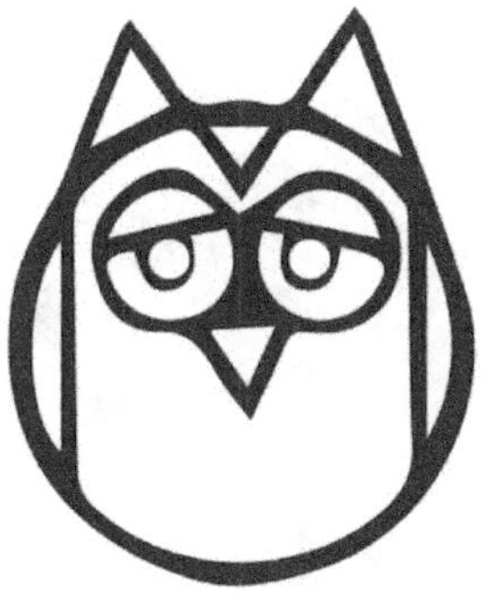

STEP 6

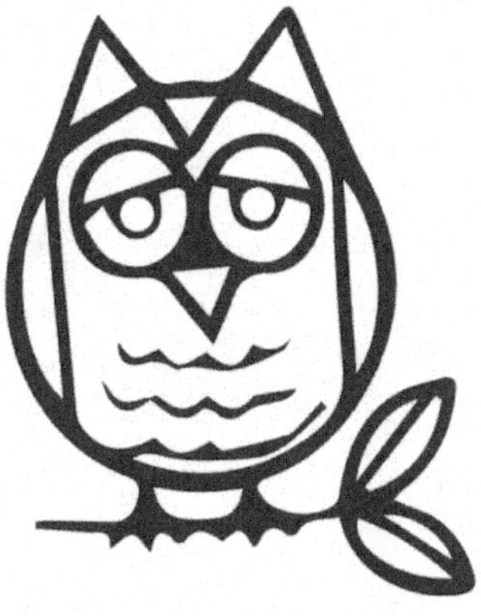

HOW TO DRAW

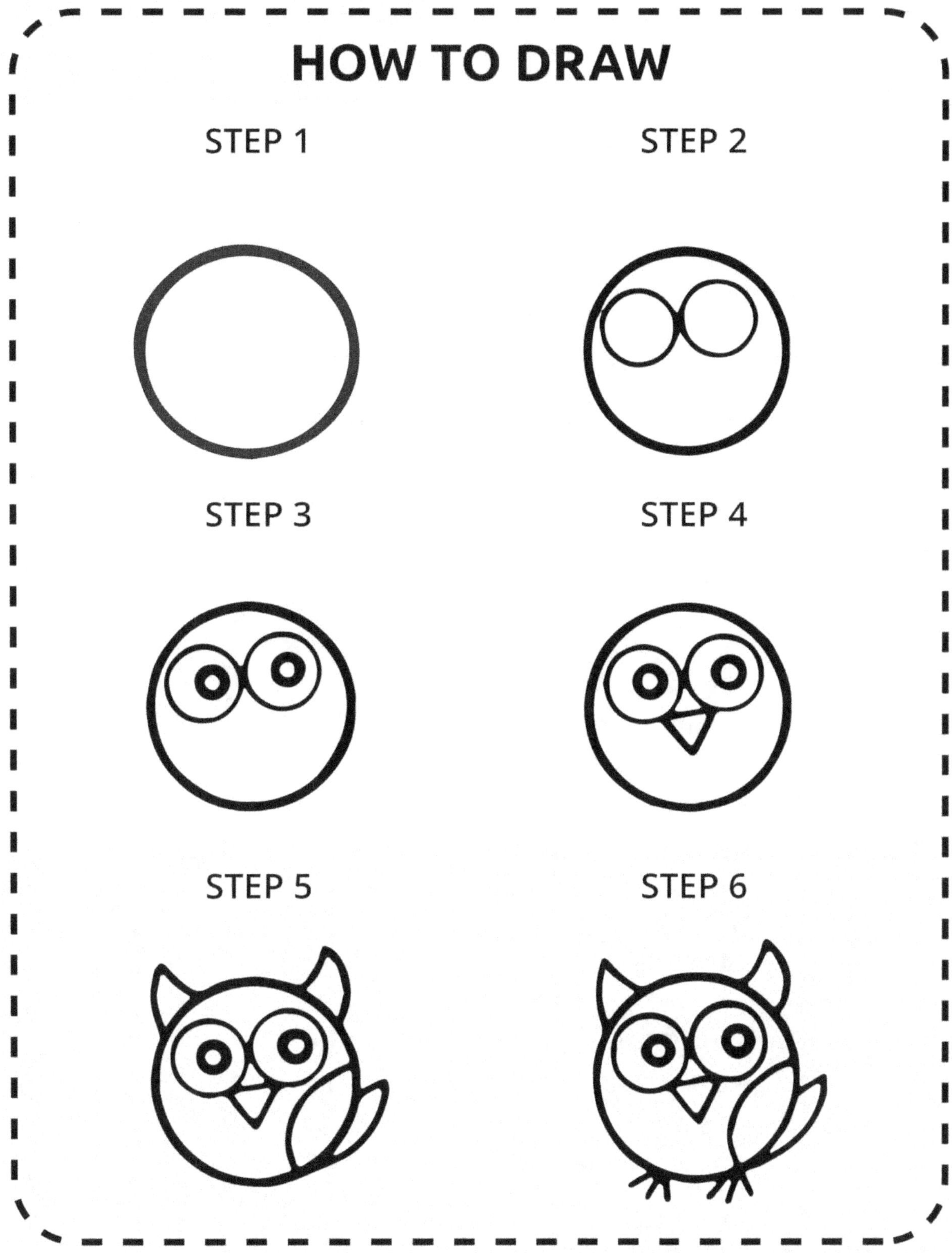

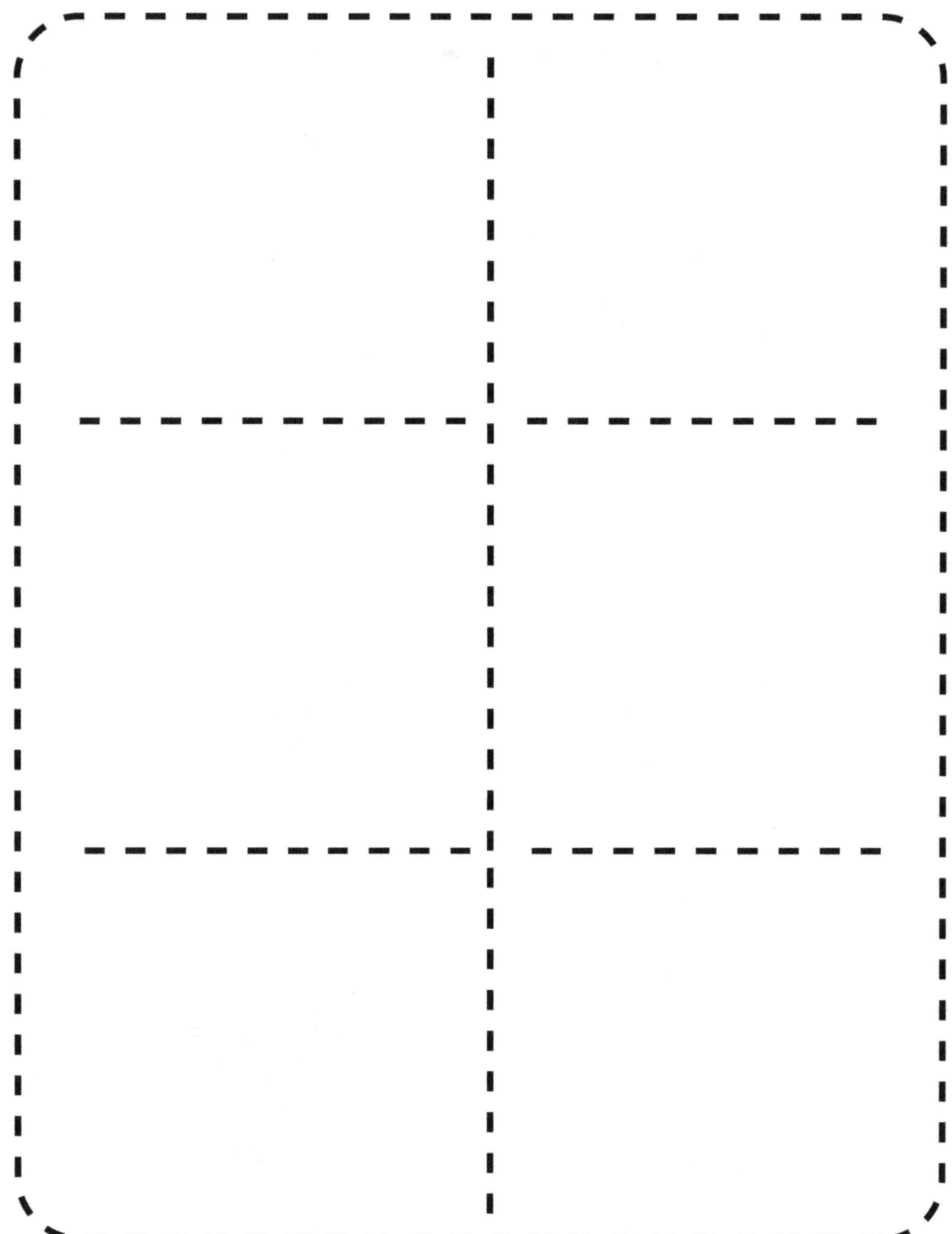

HOW TO DRAW

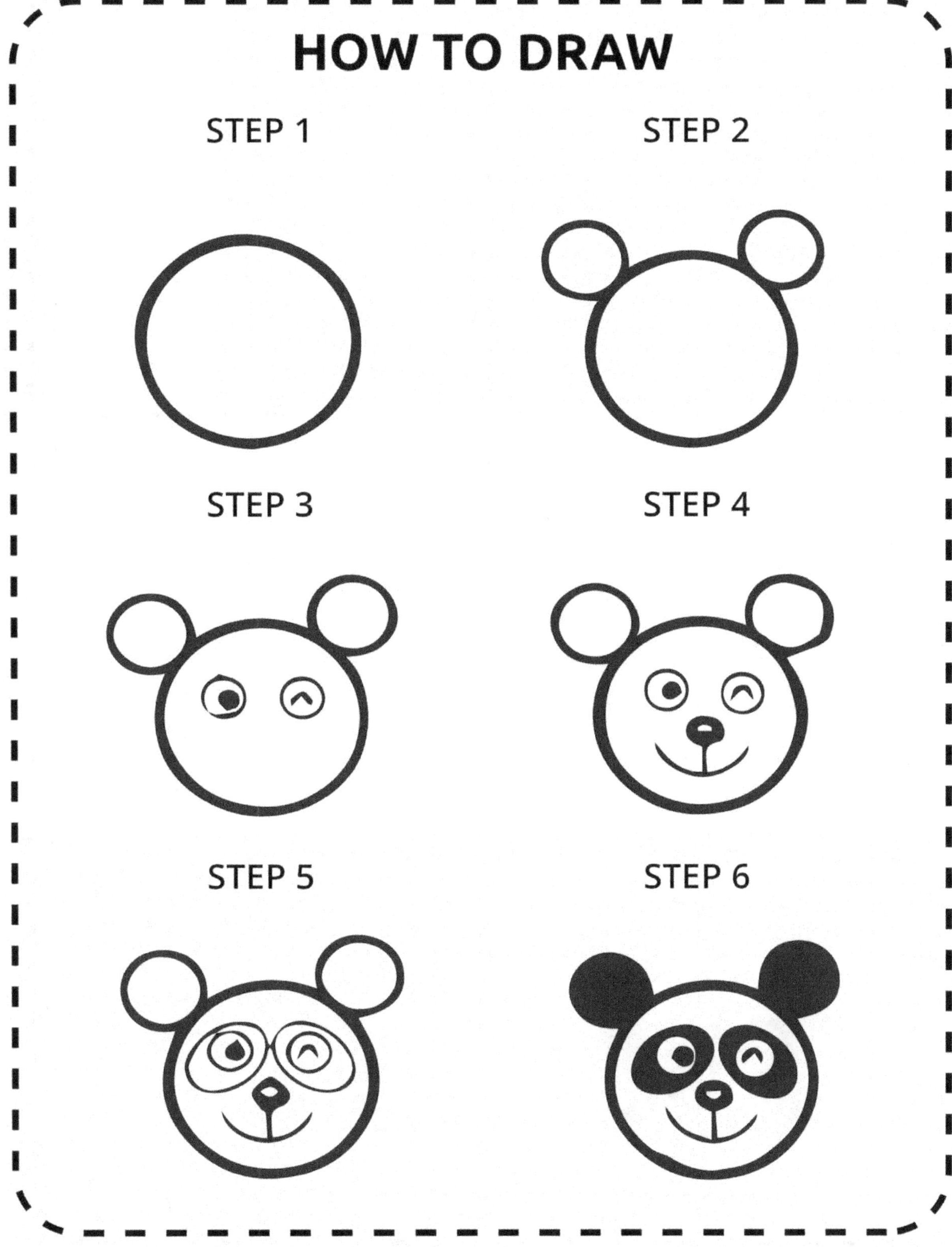

HOW TO DRAW

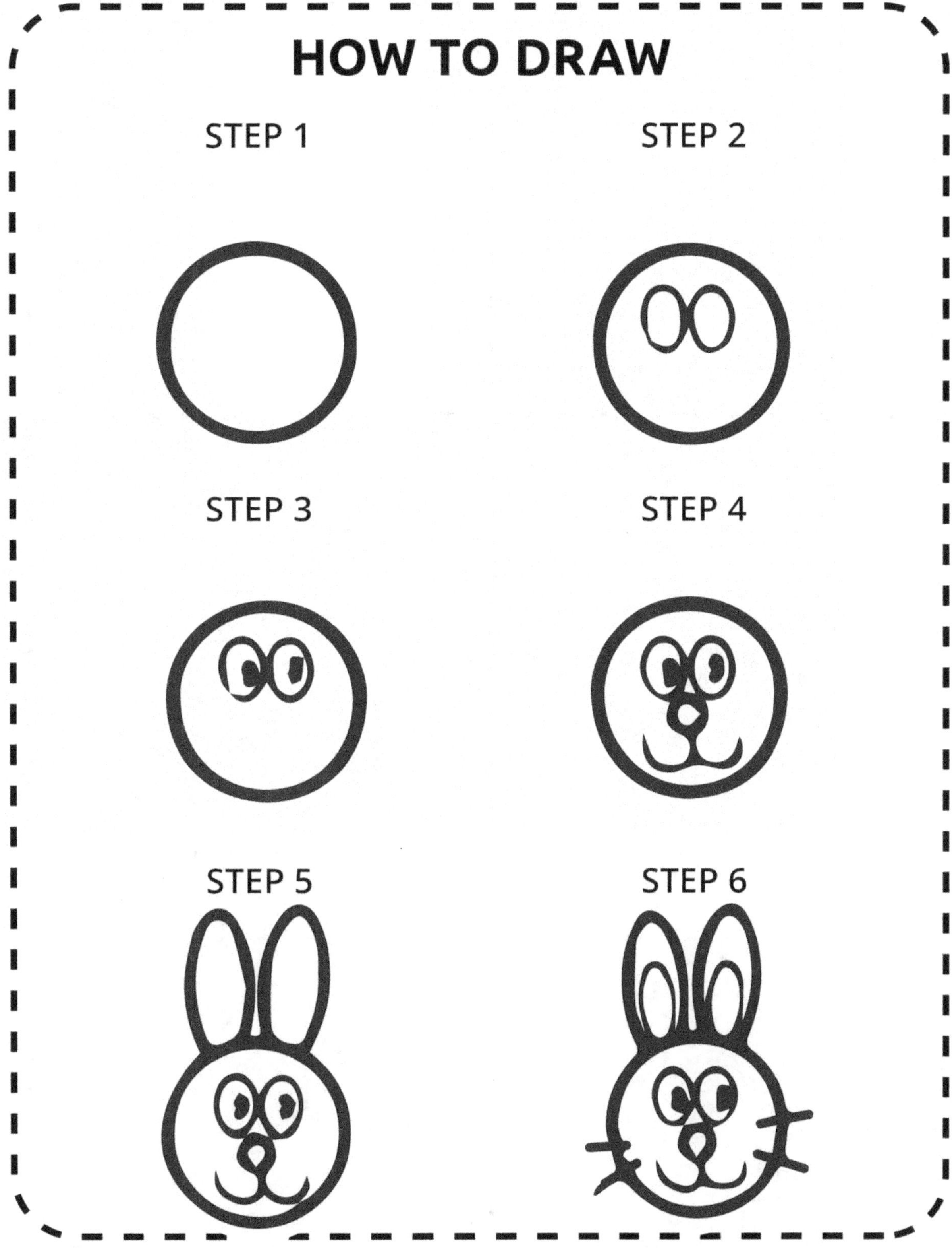

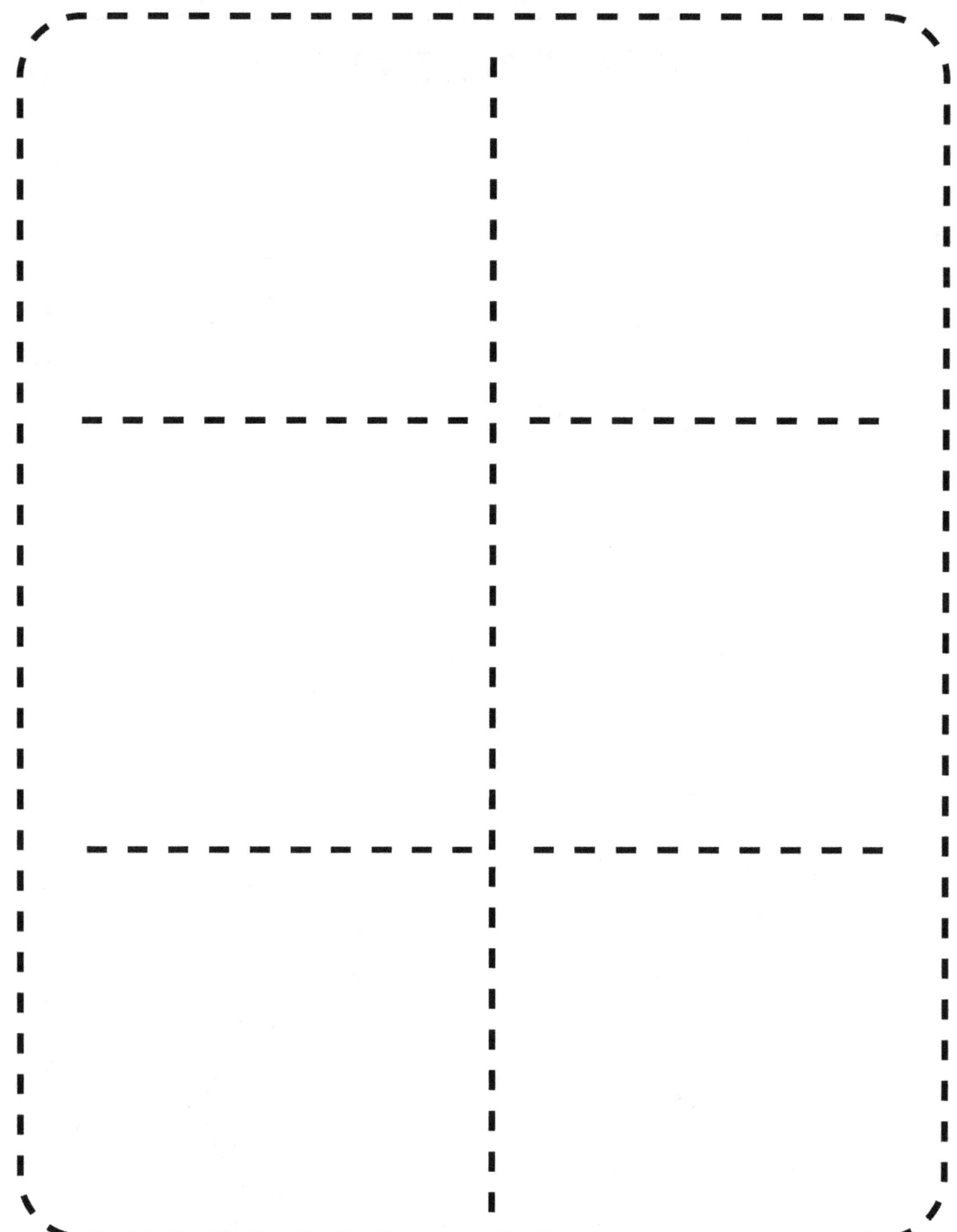

HOW TO DRAW

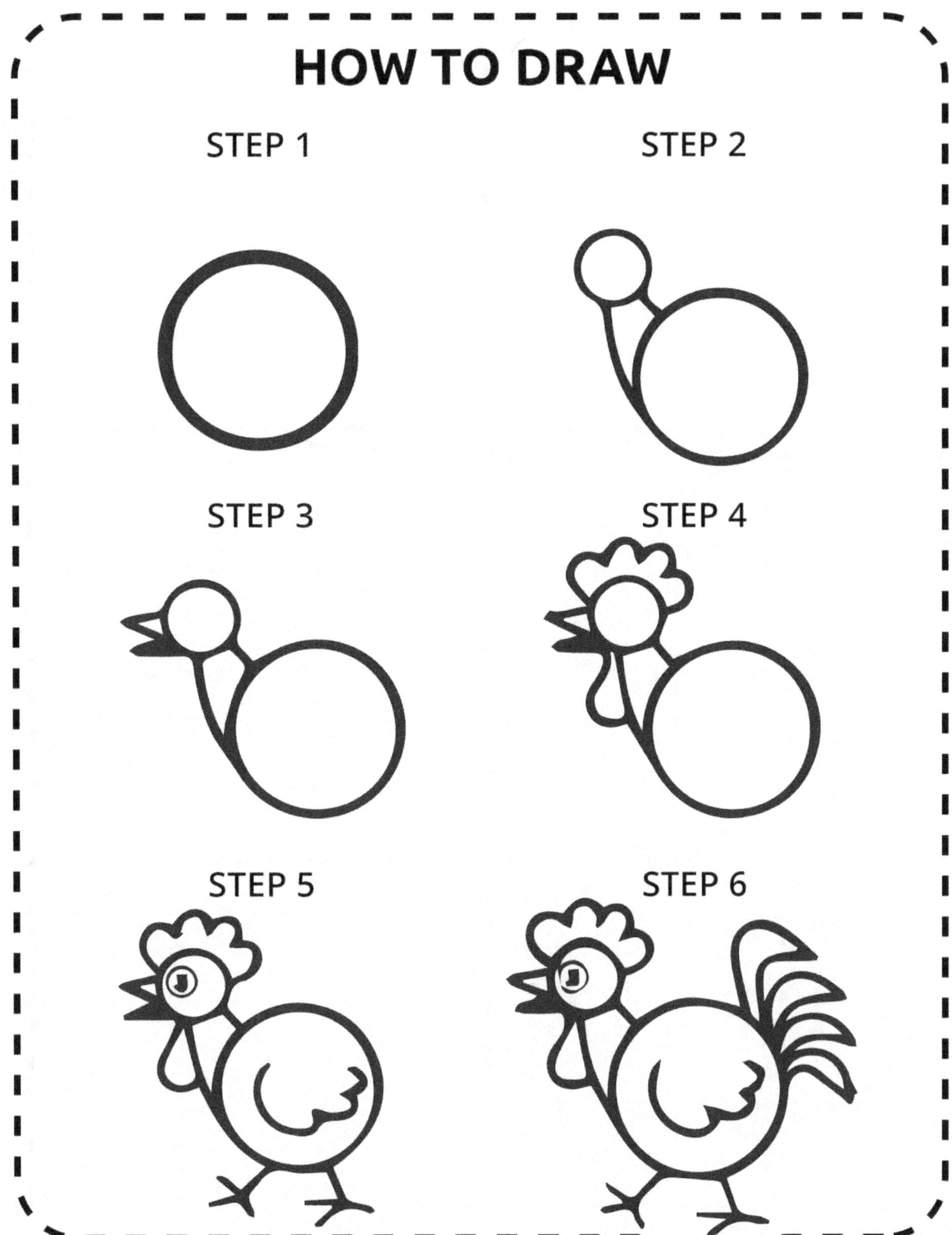

HOW TO DRAW

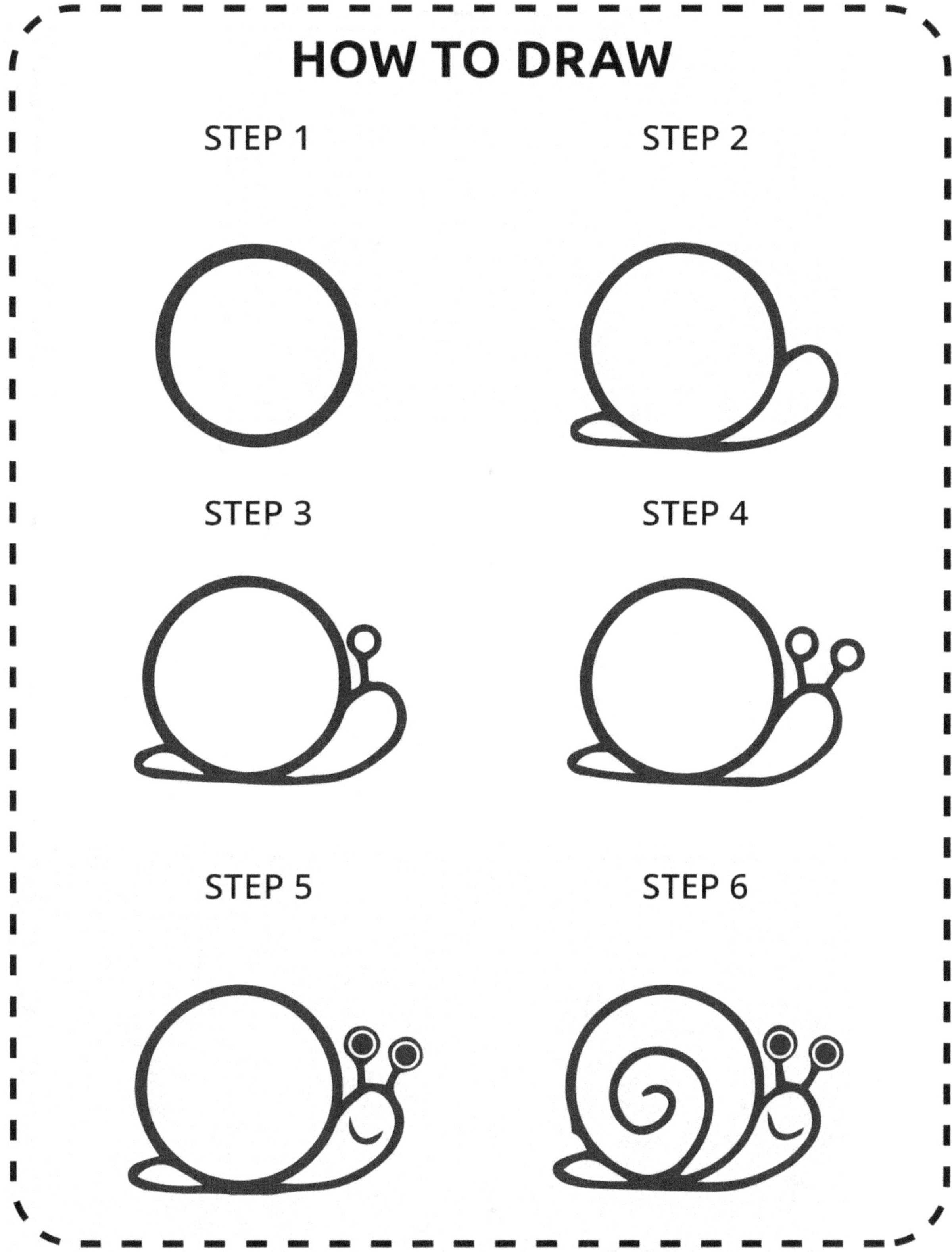

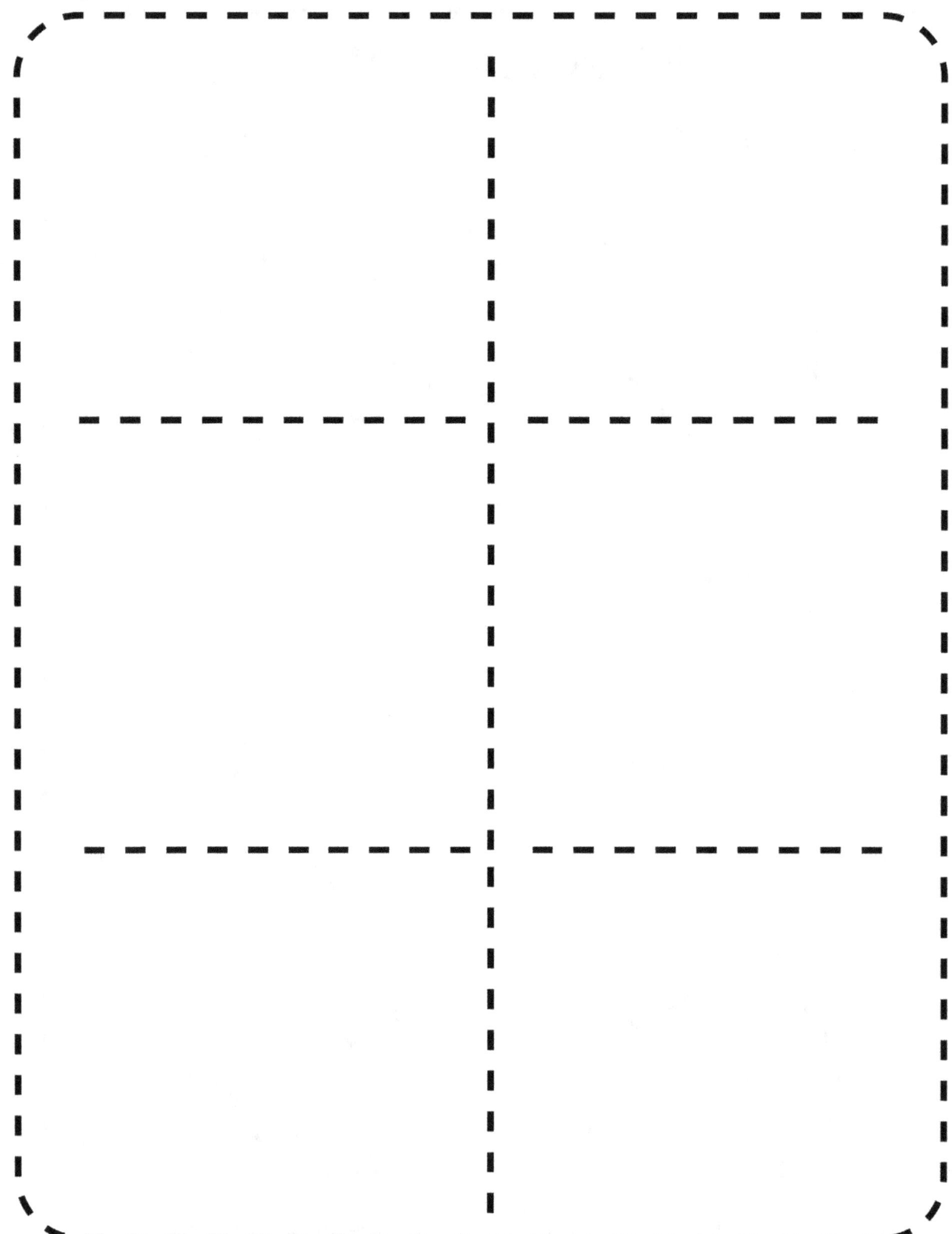

HOW TO DRAW

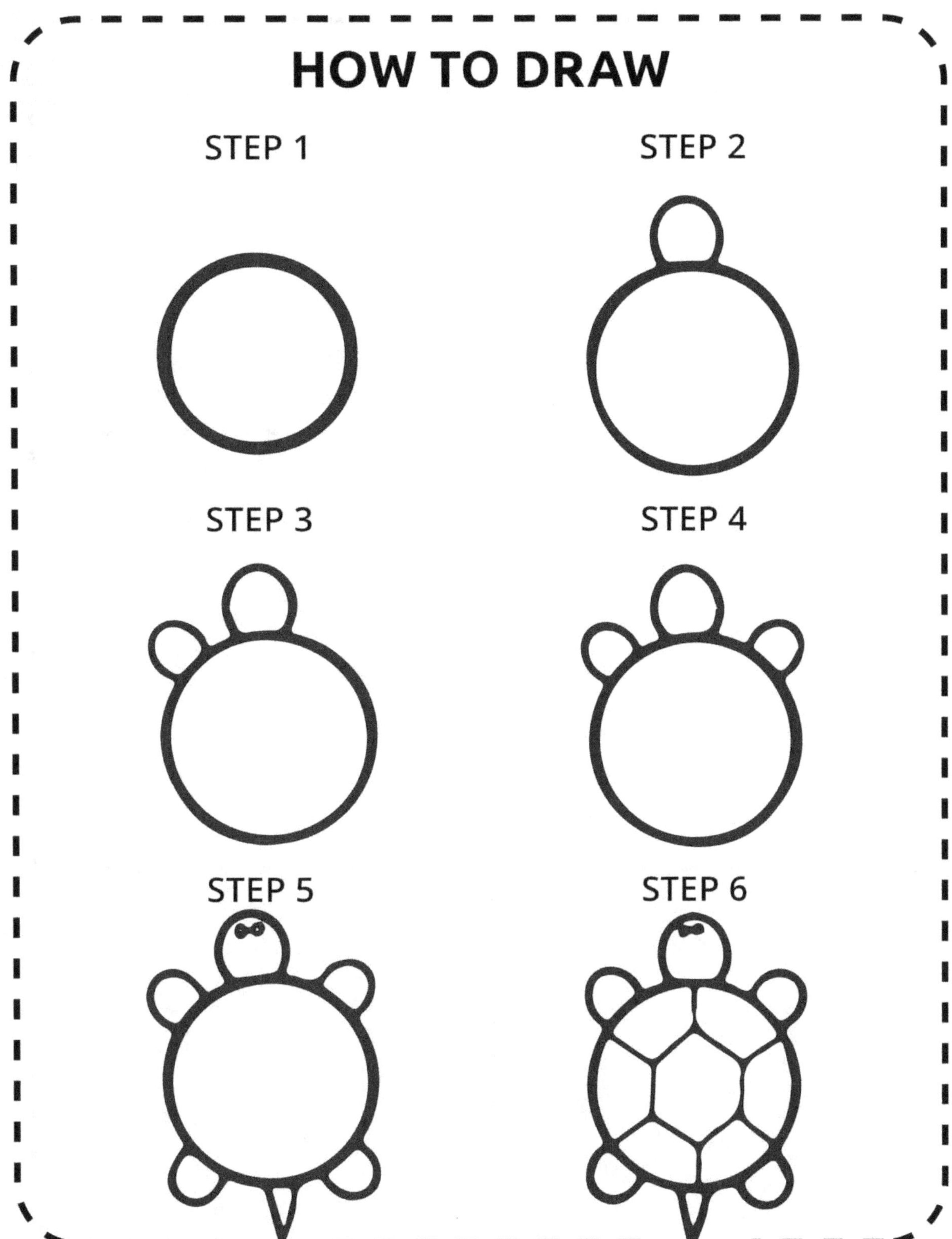

HOW TO DRAW

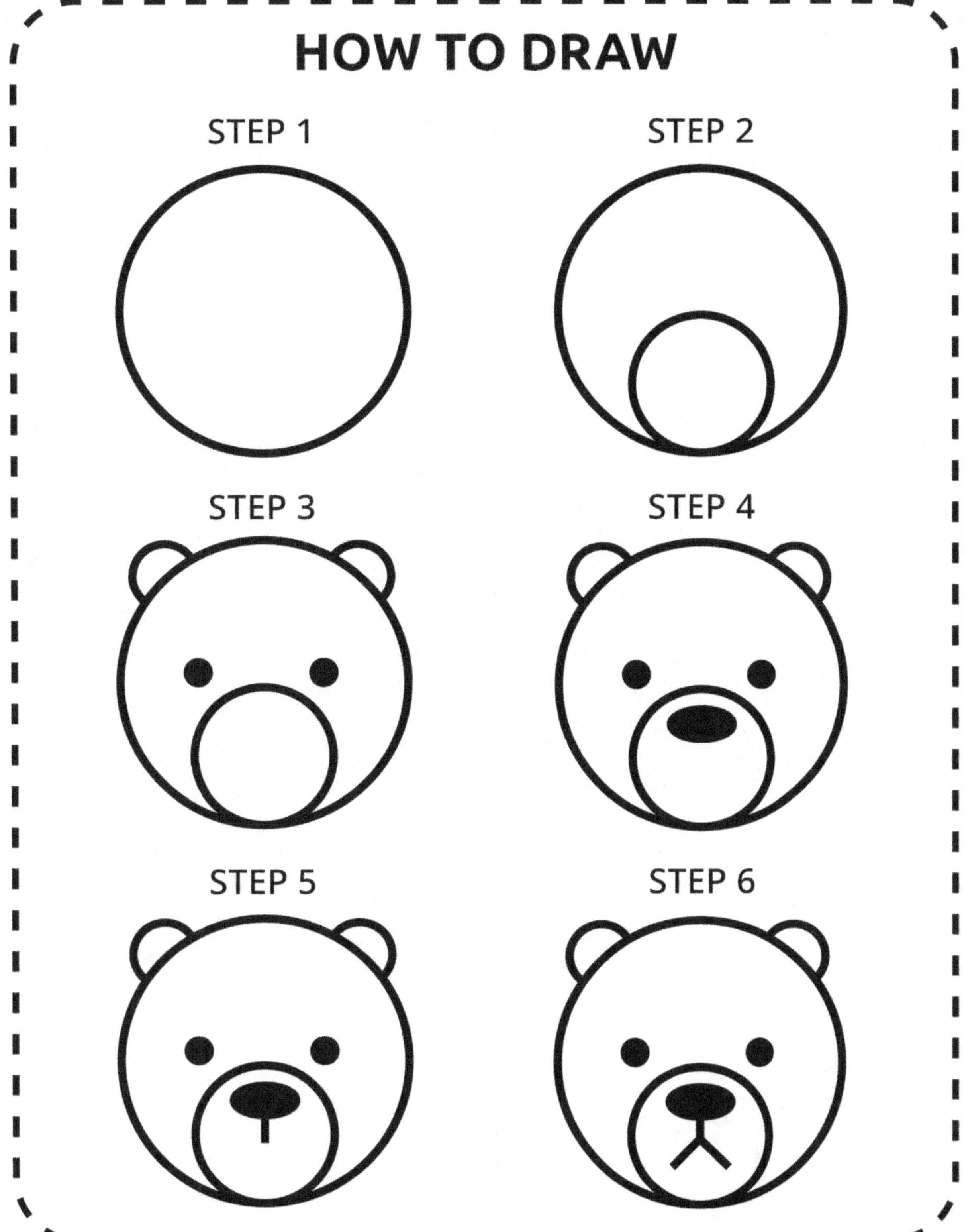

HOW TO DRAW

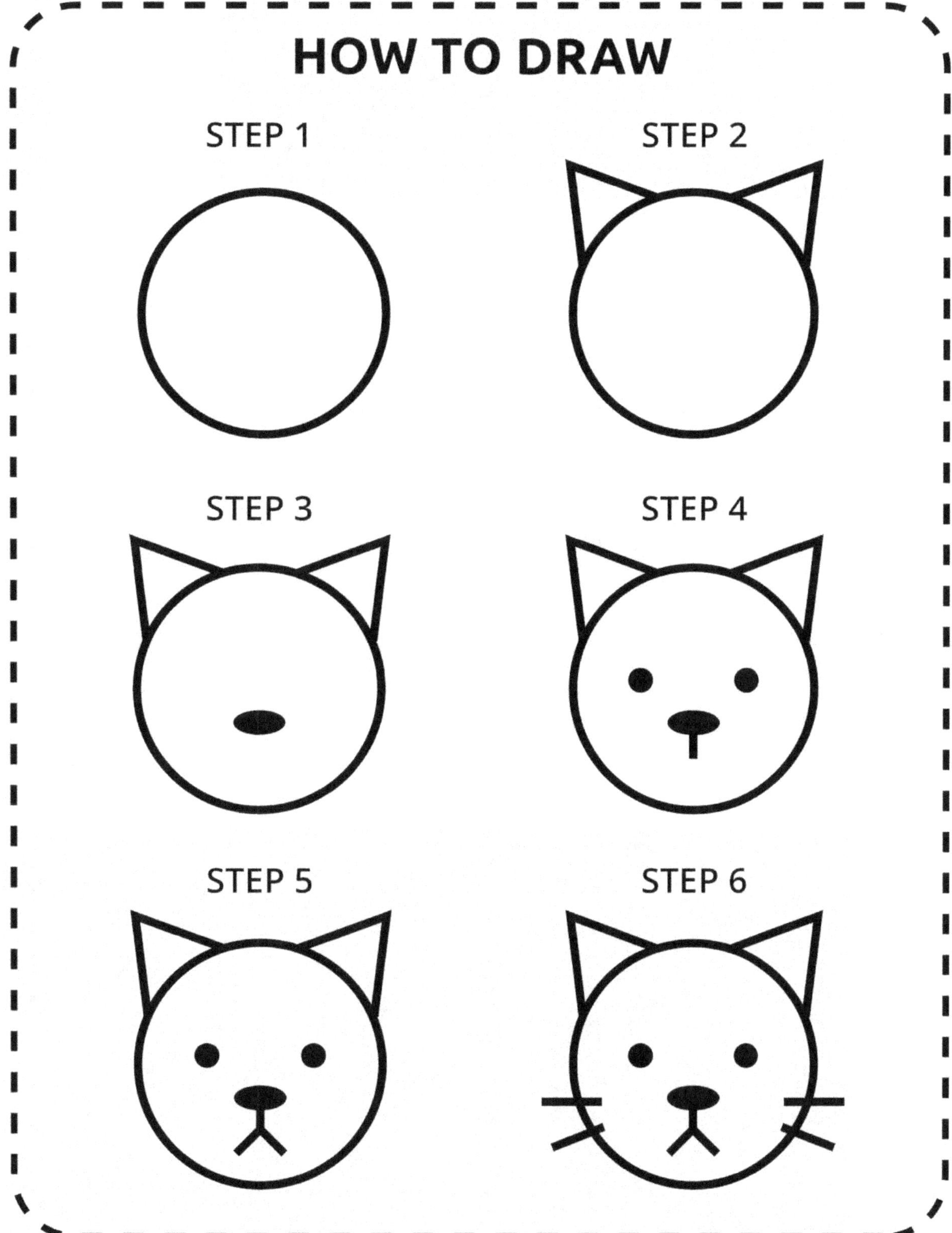

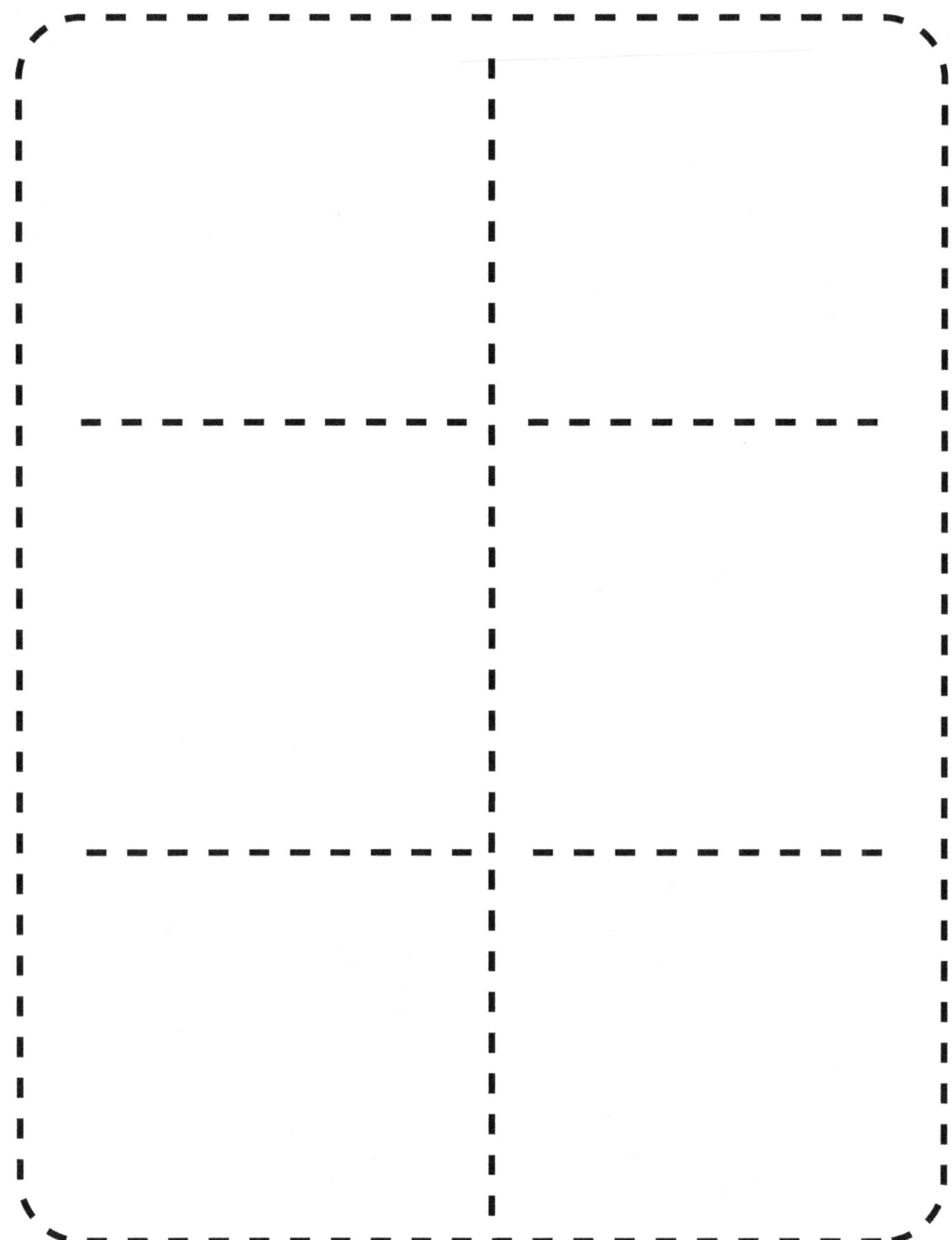

HOW TO DRAW

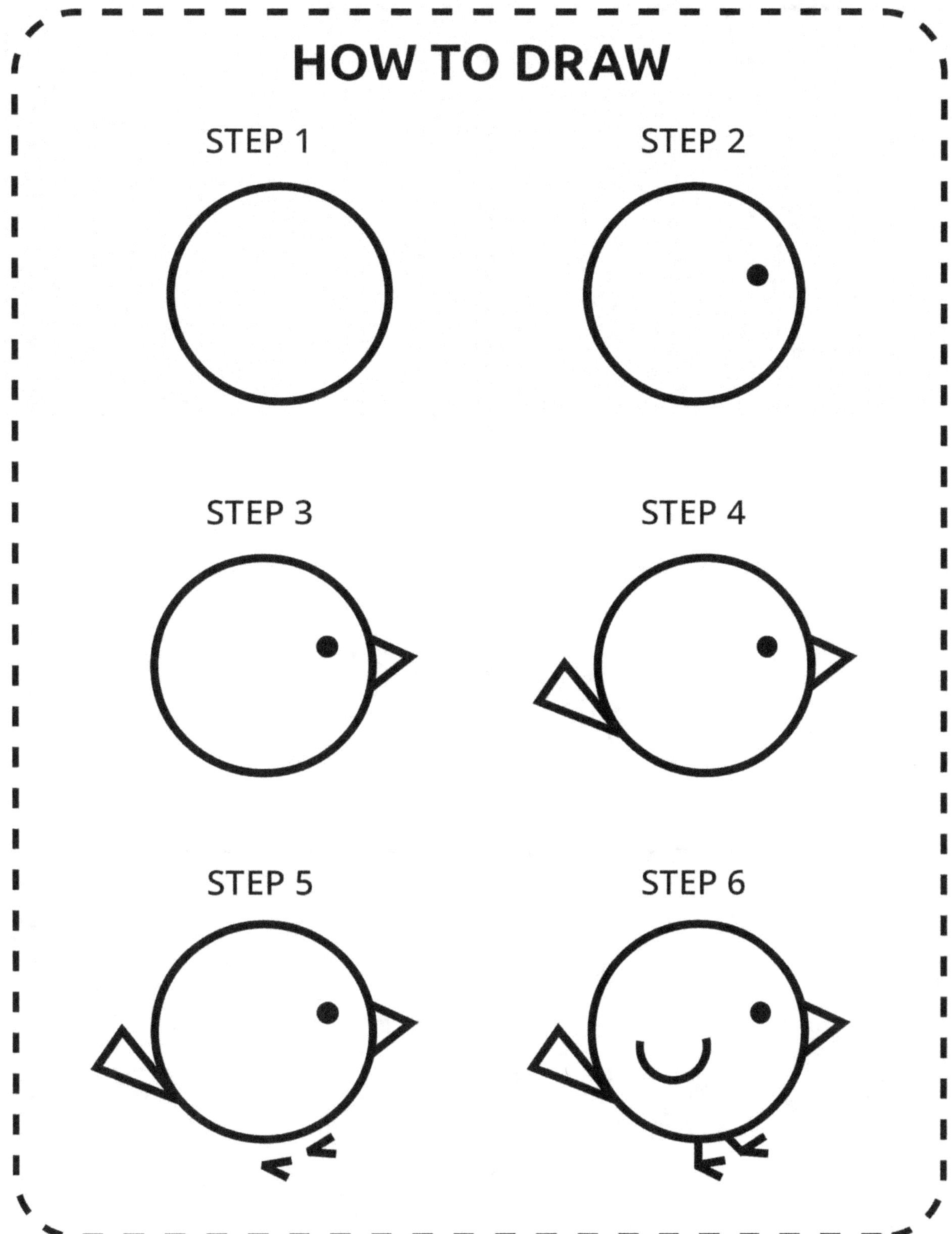

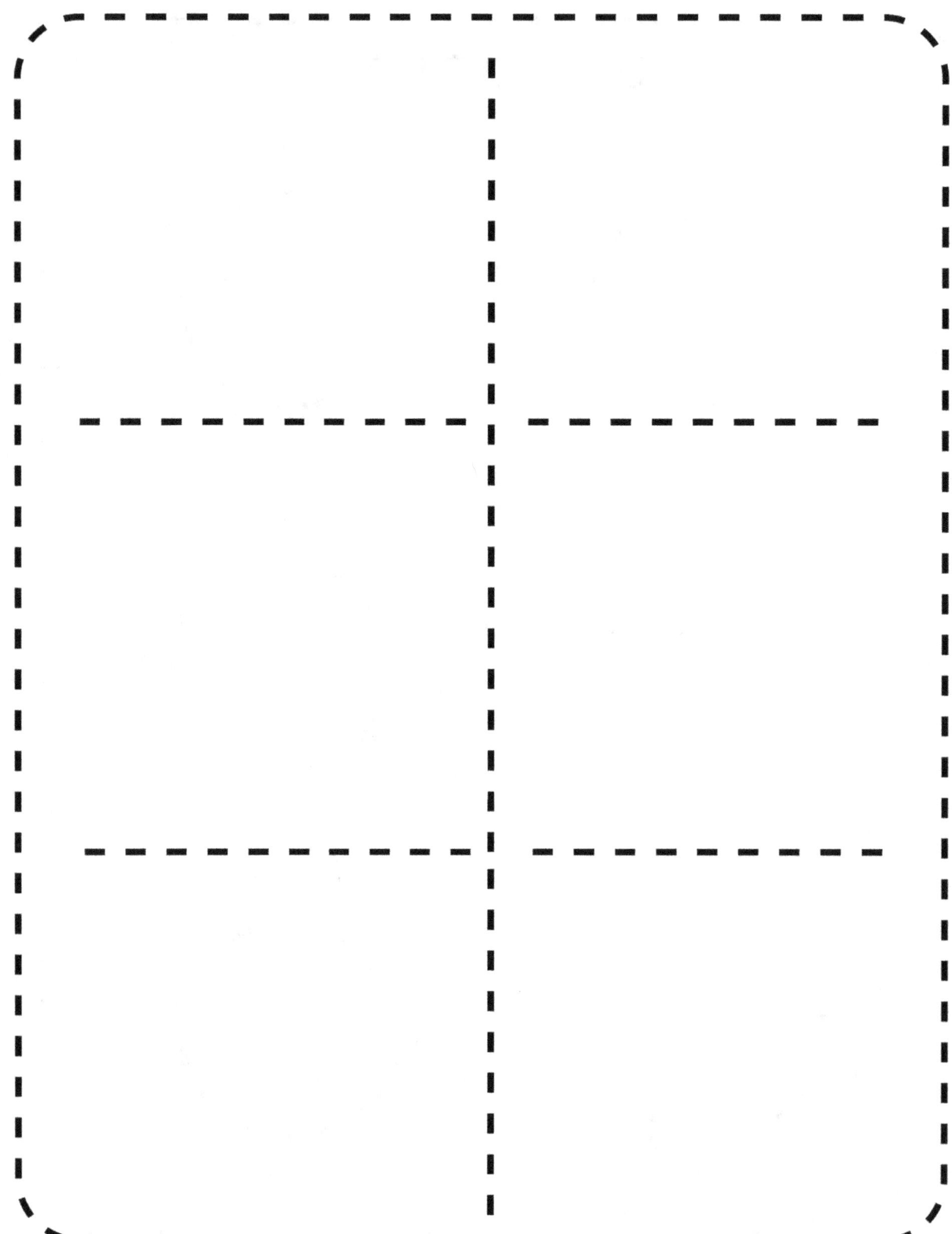

HOW TO DRAW

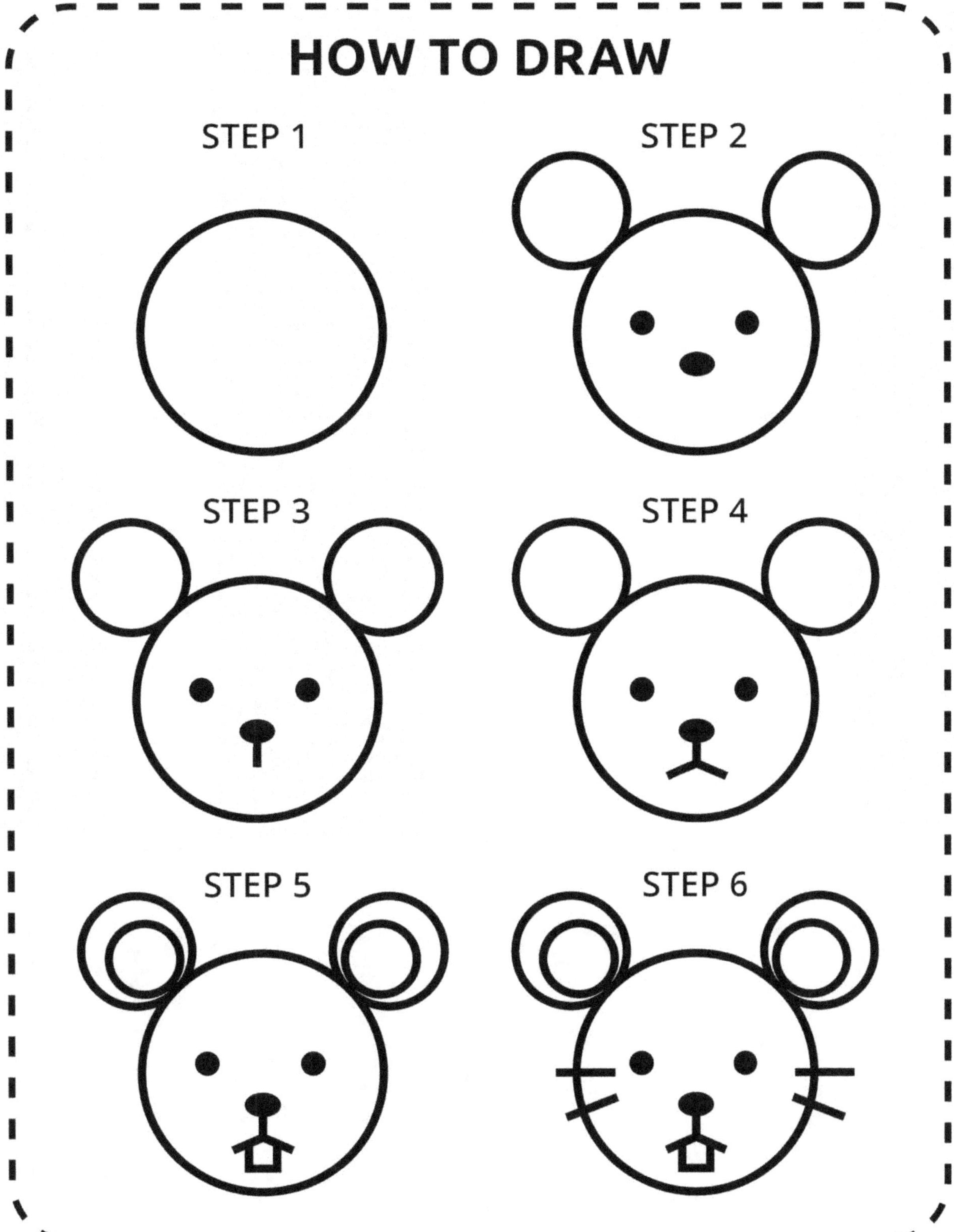

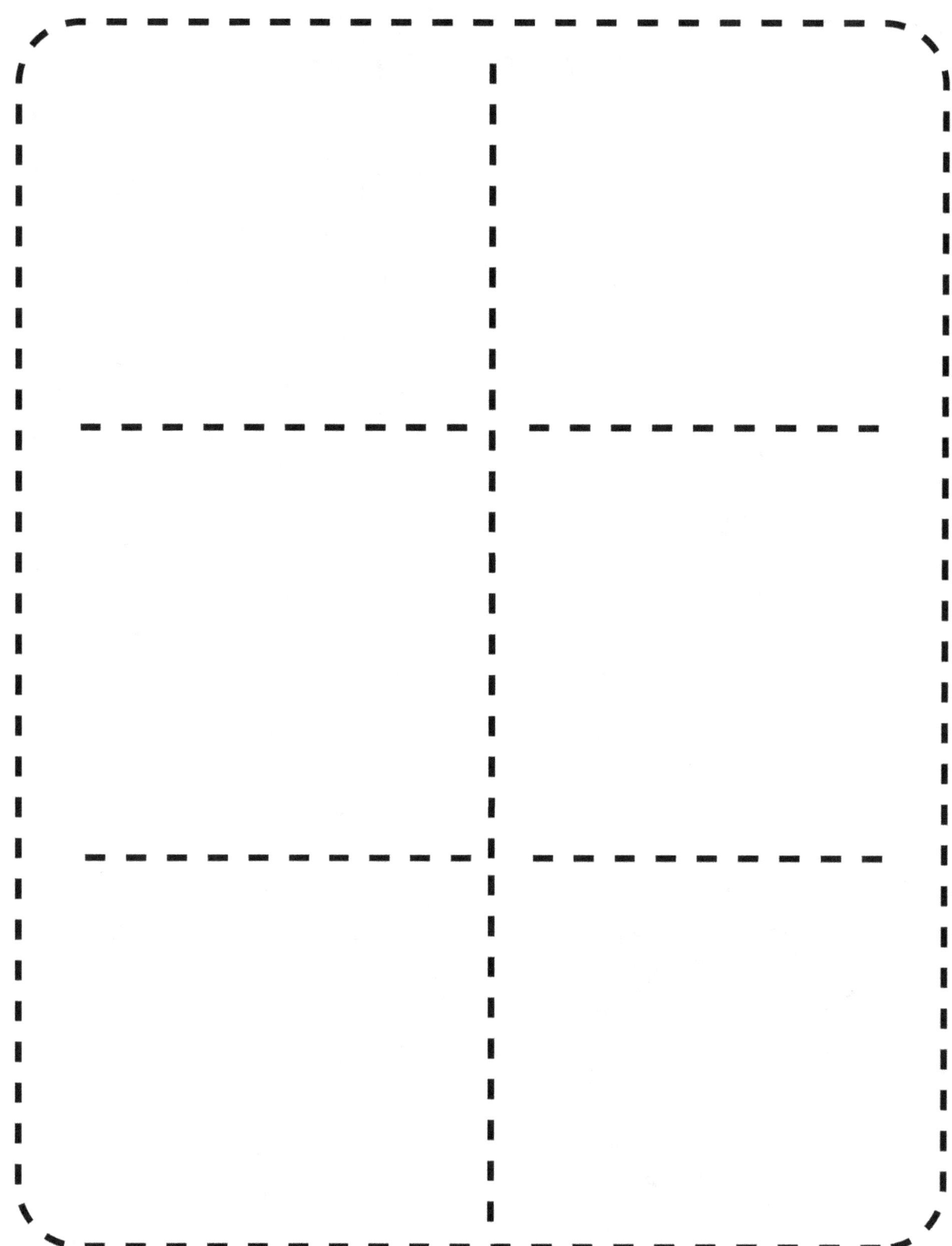

HOW TO DRAW

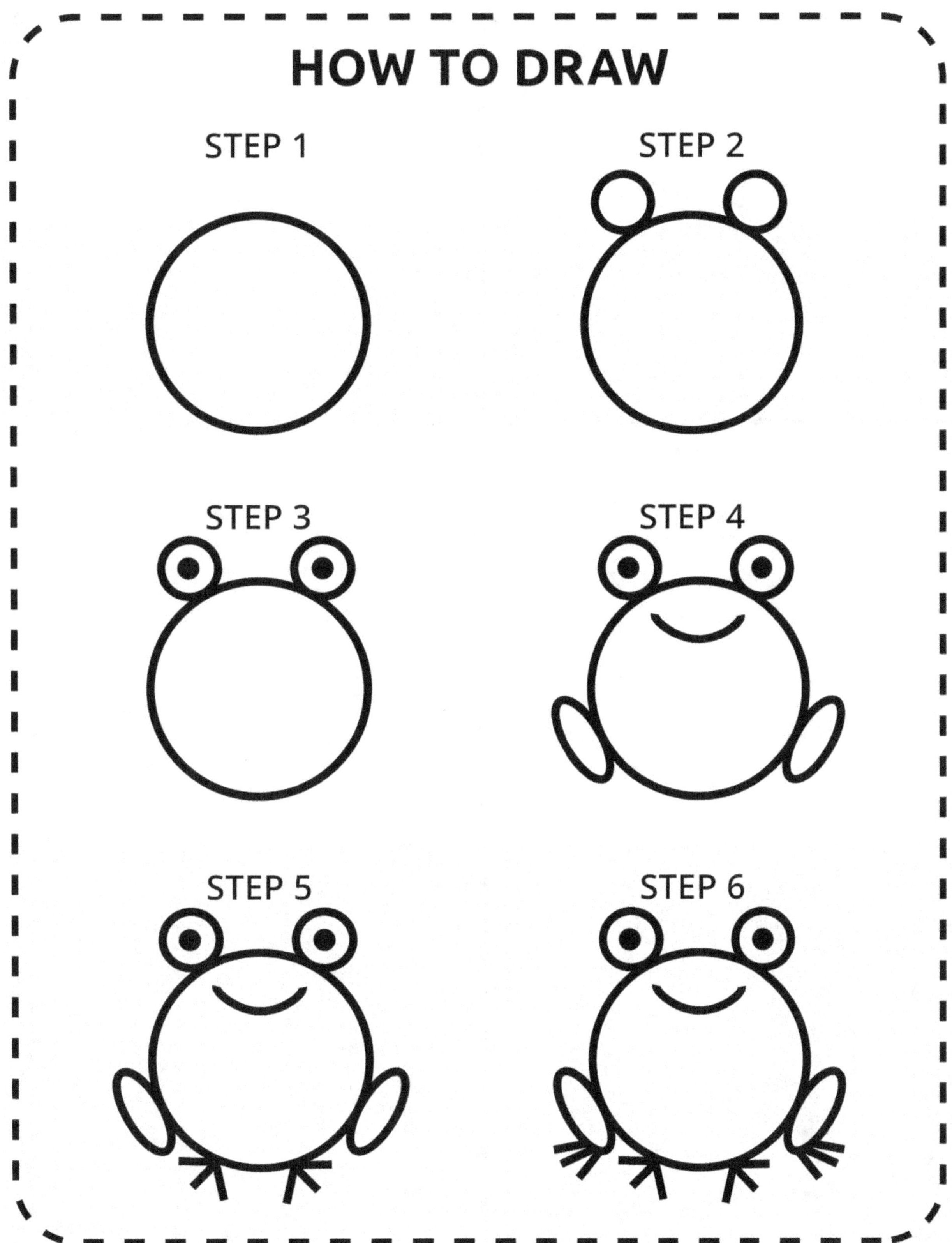

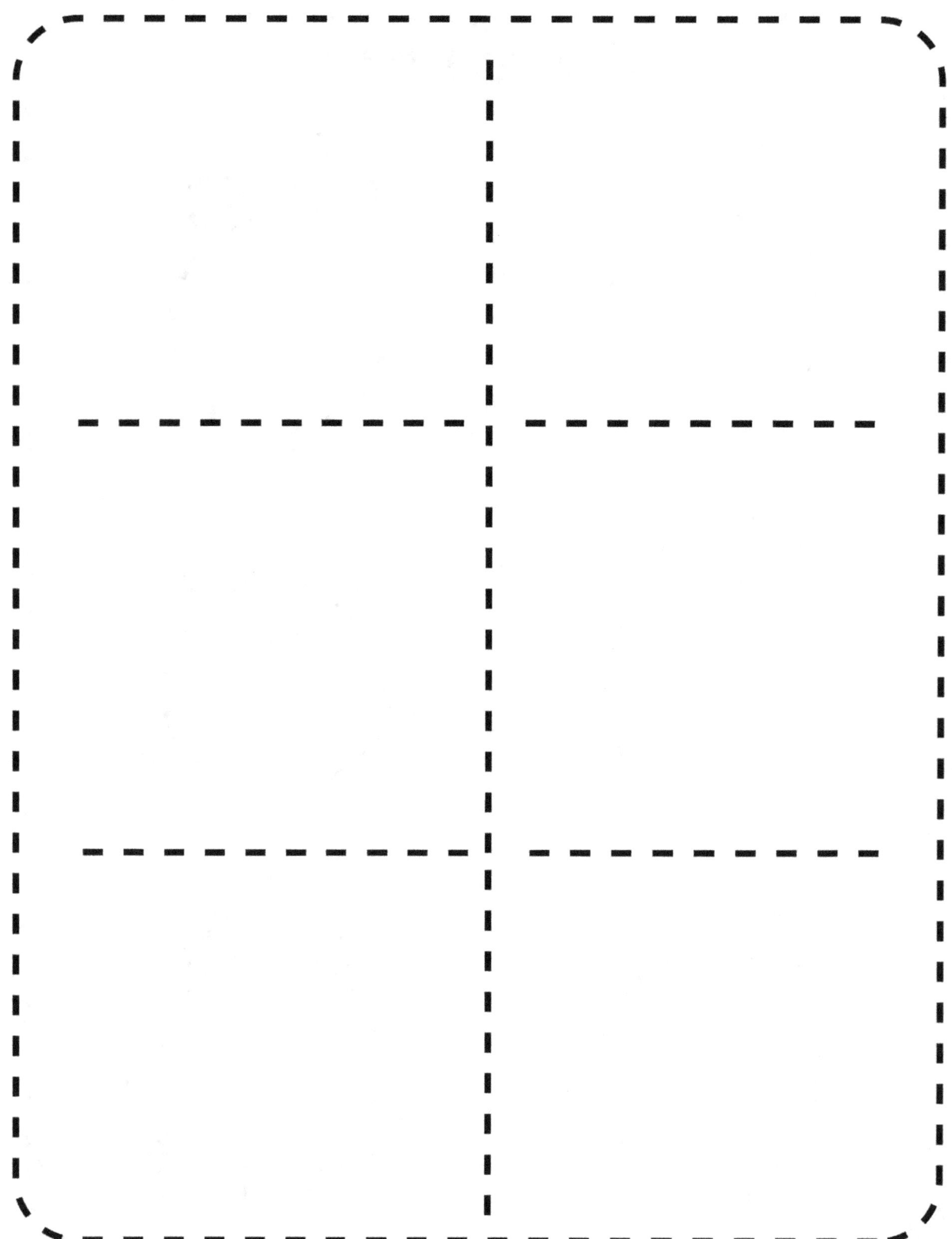

HOW TO DRAW

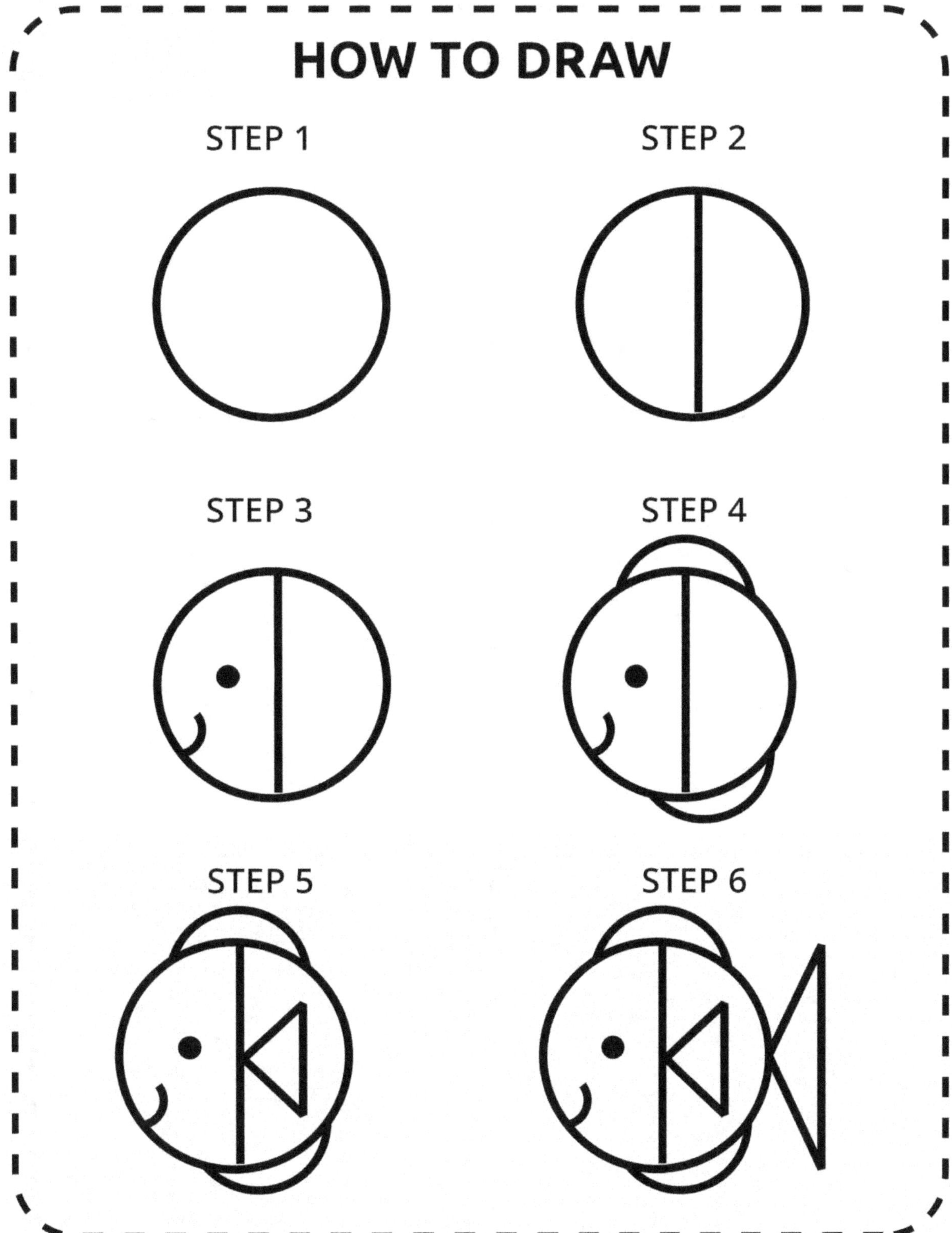

HOW TO DRAW

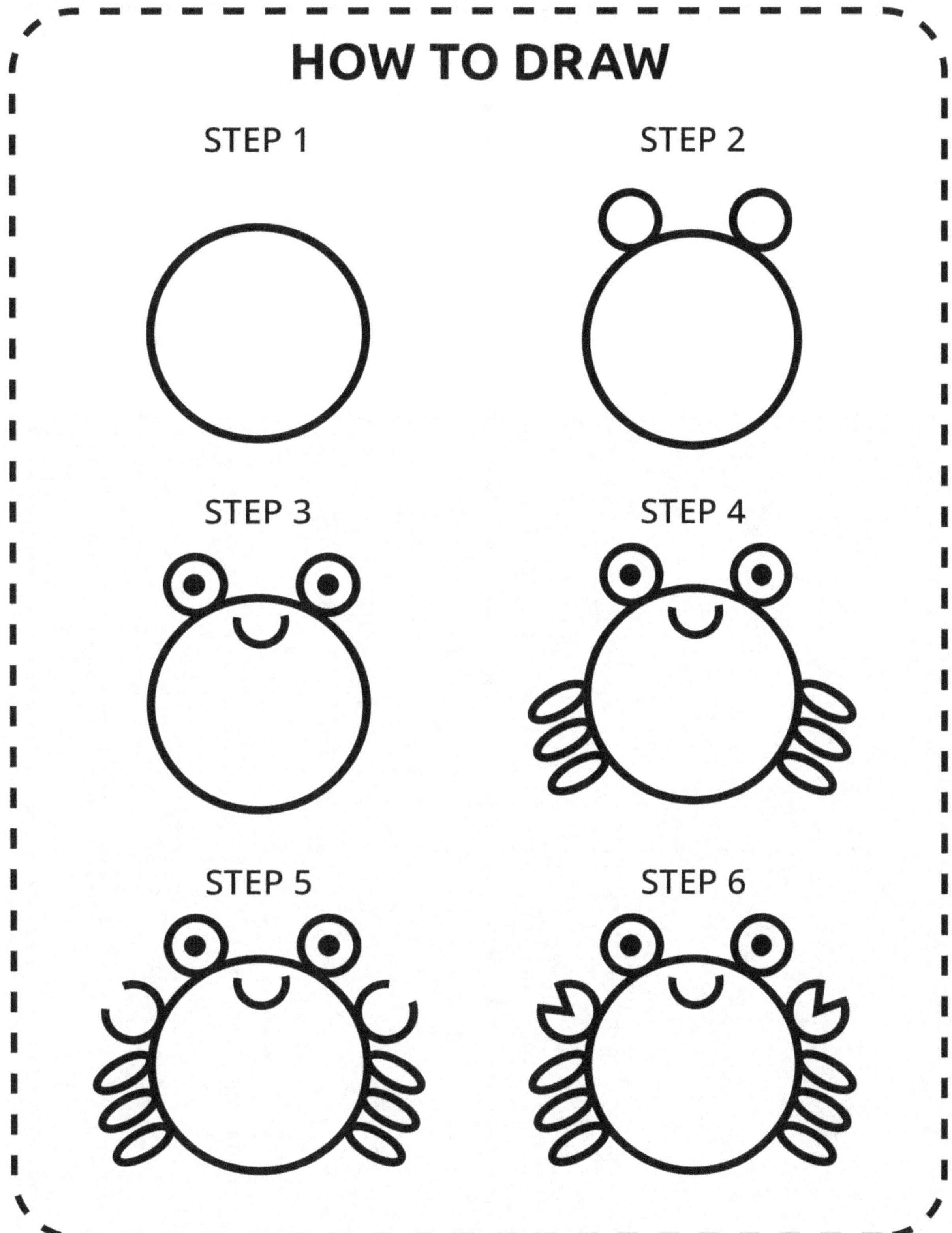

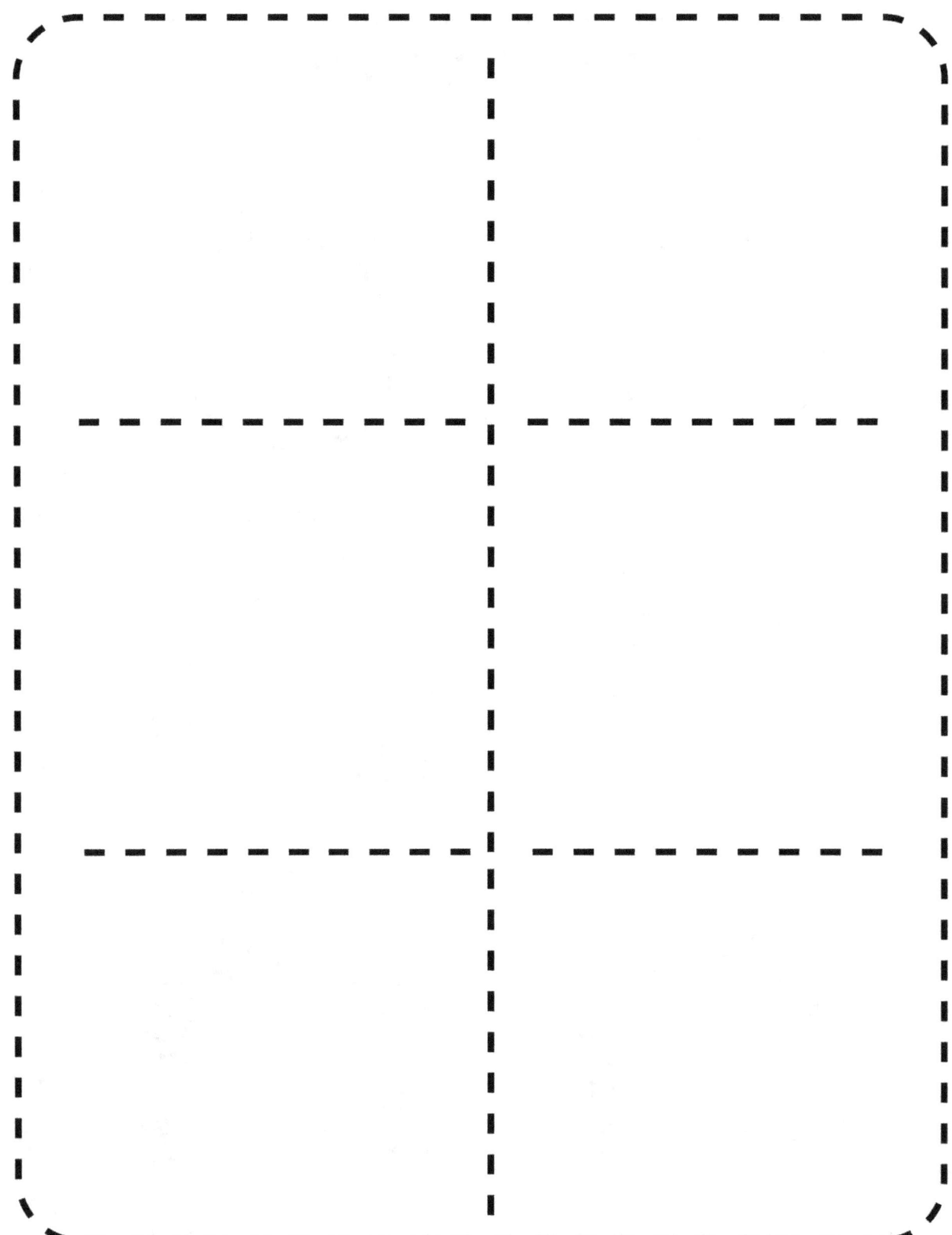

HOW TO DRAW

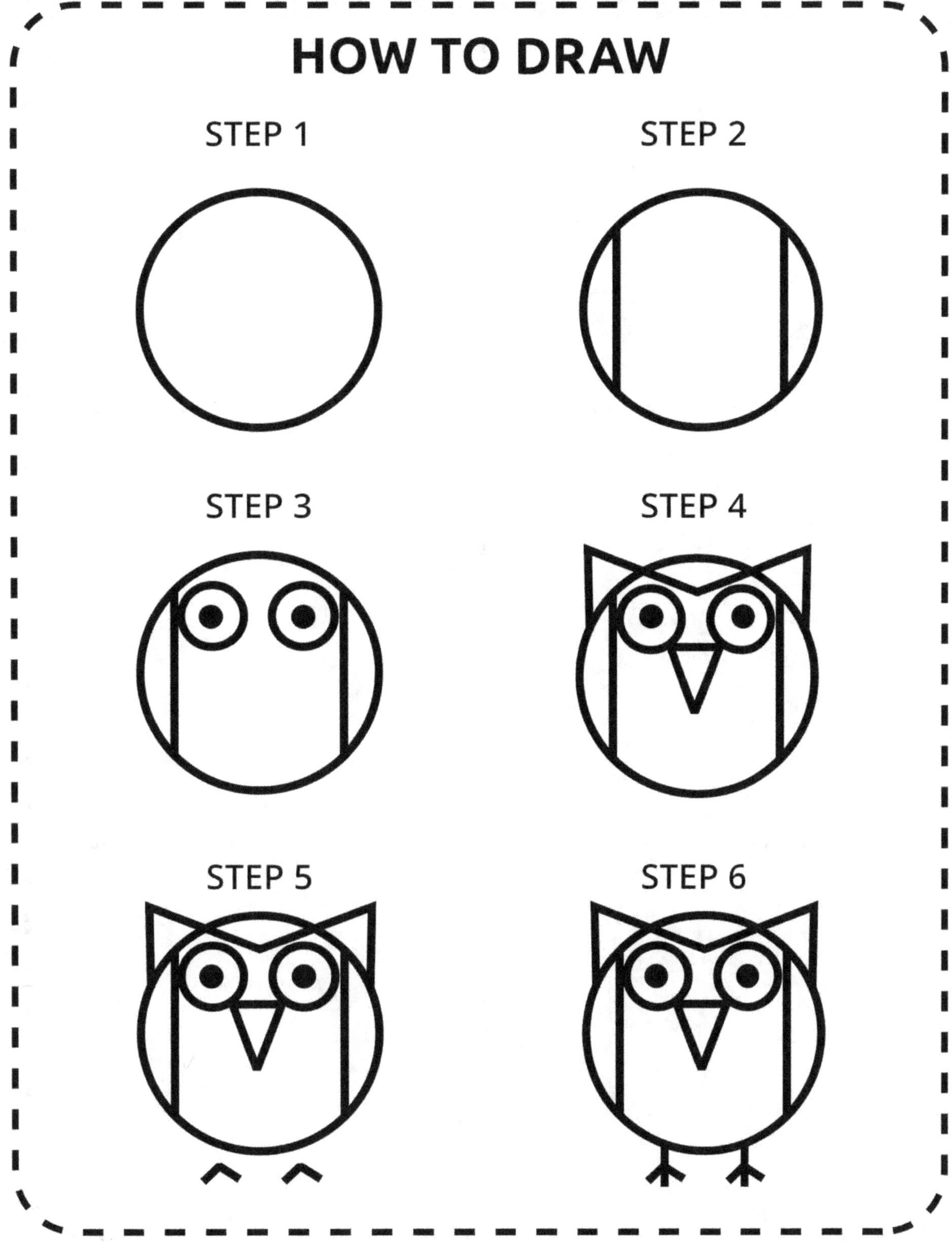

HOW TO DRAW

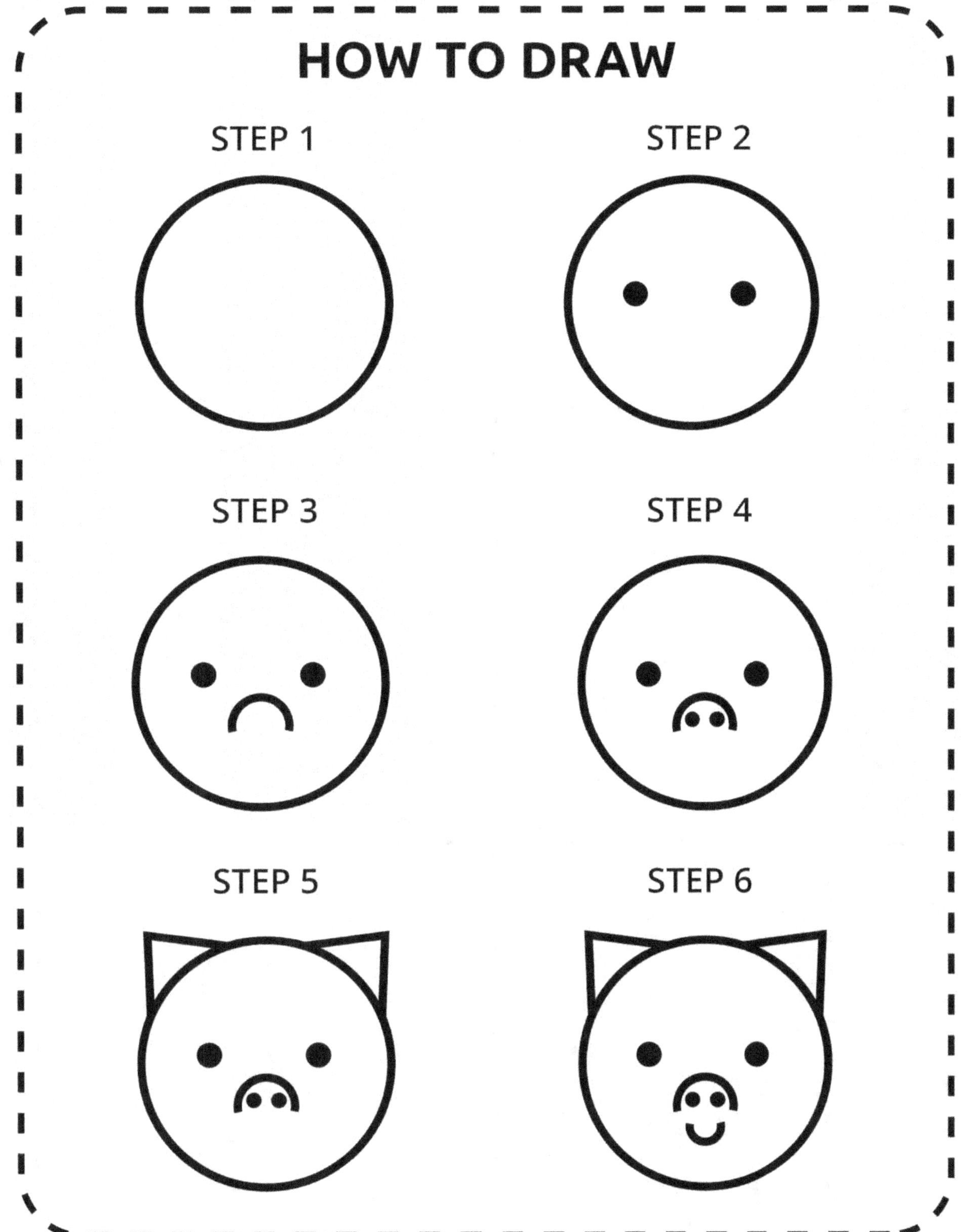

HOW TO DRAW

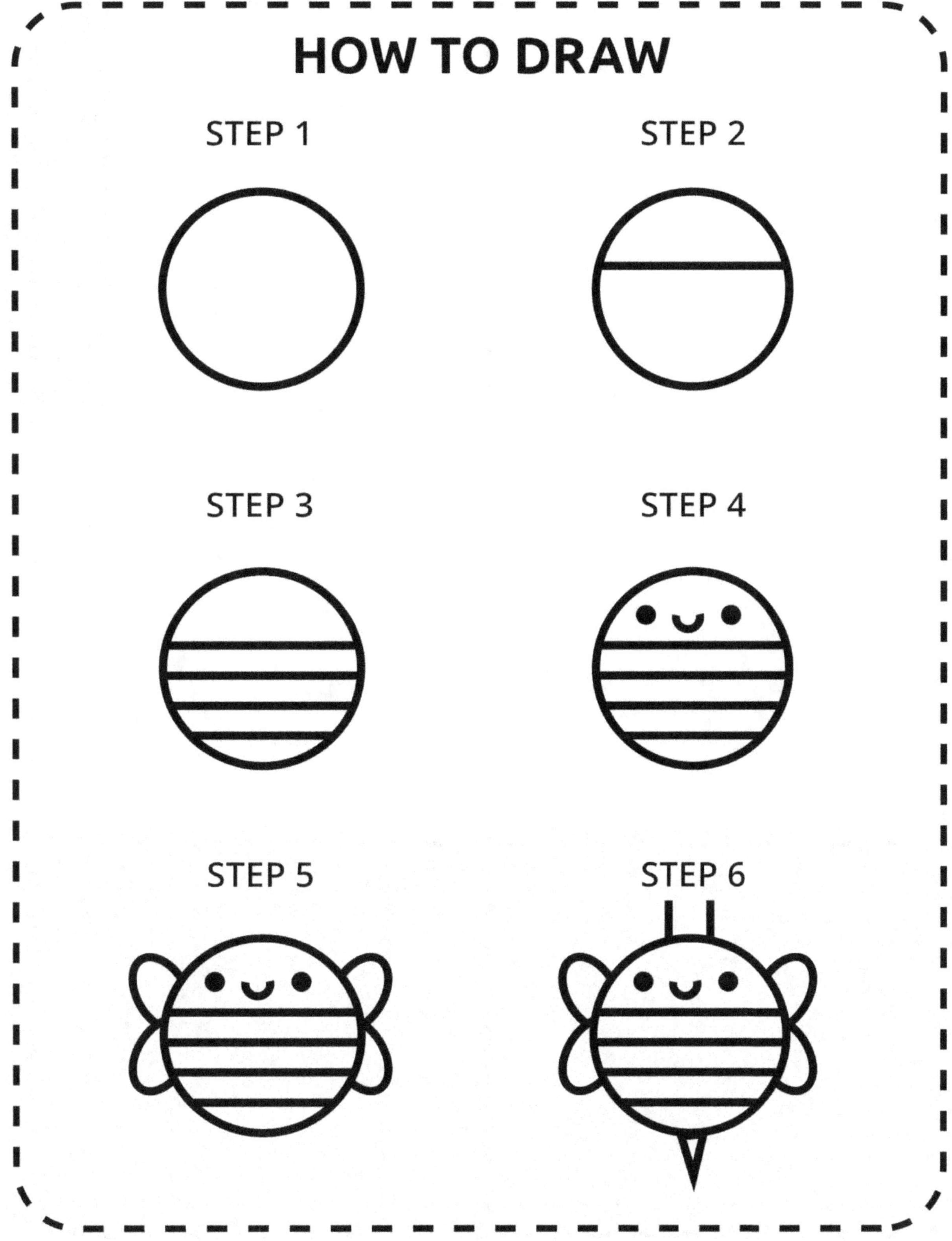

HOW TO DRAW

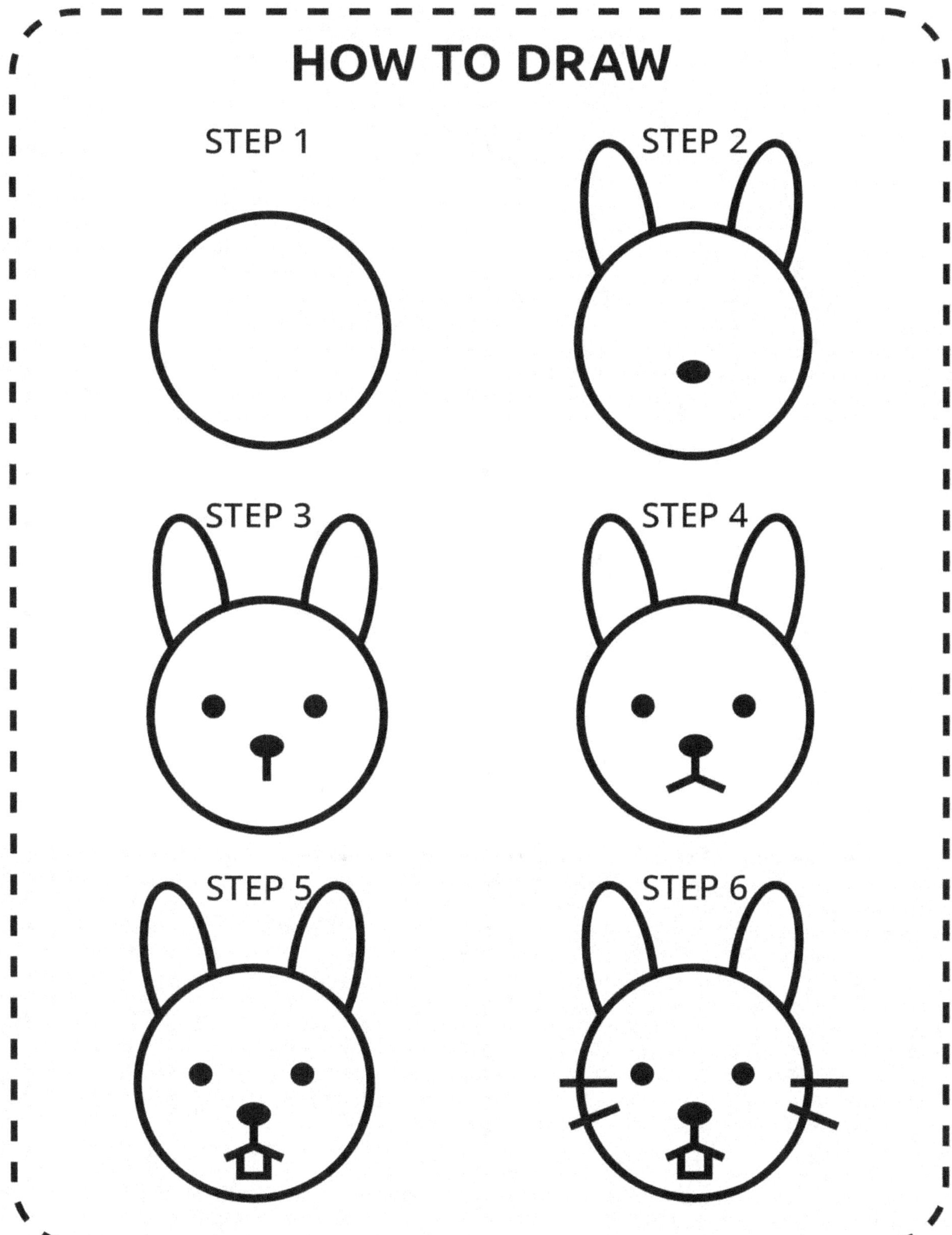

HOW TO DRAW

STEP 1

STEP 2

STEP 3

STEP 4

STEP 5

STEP 6

HOW TO DRAW

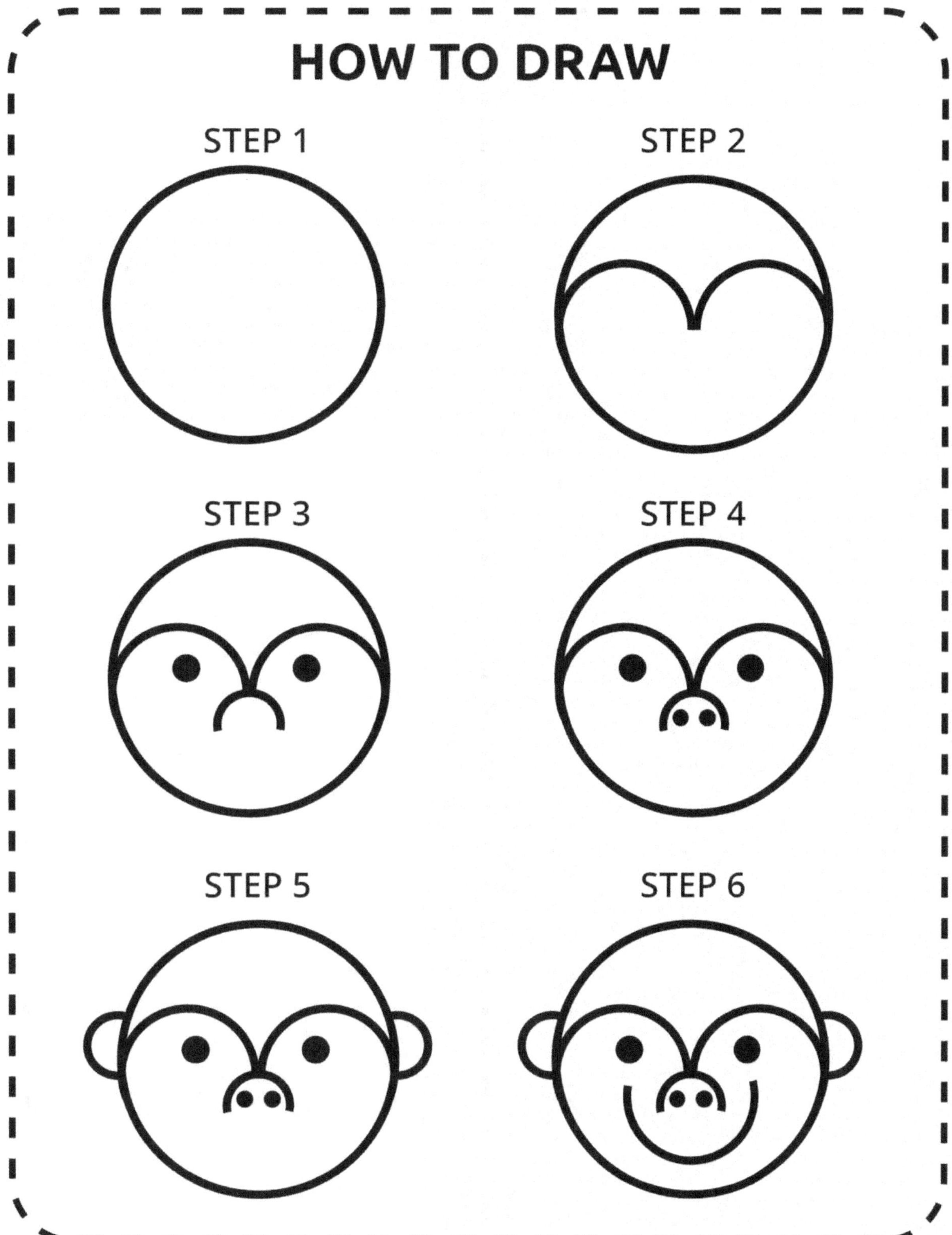

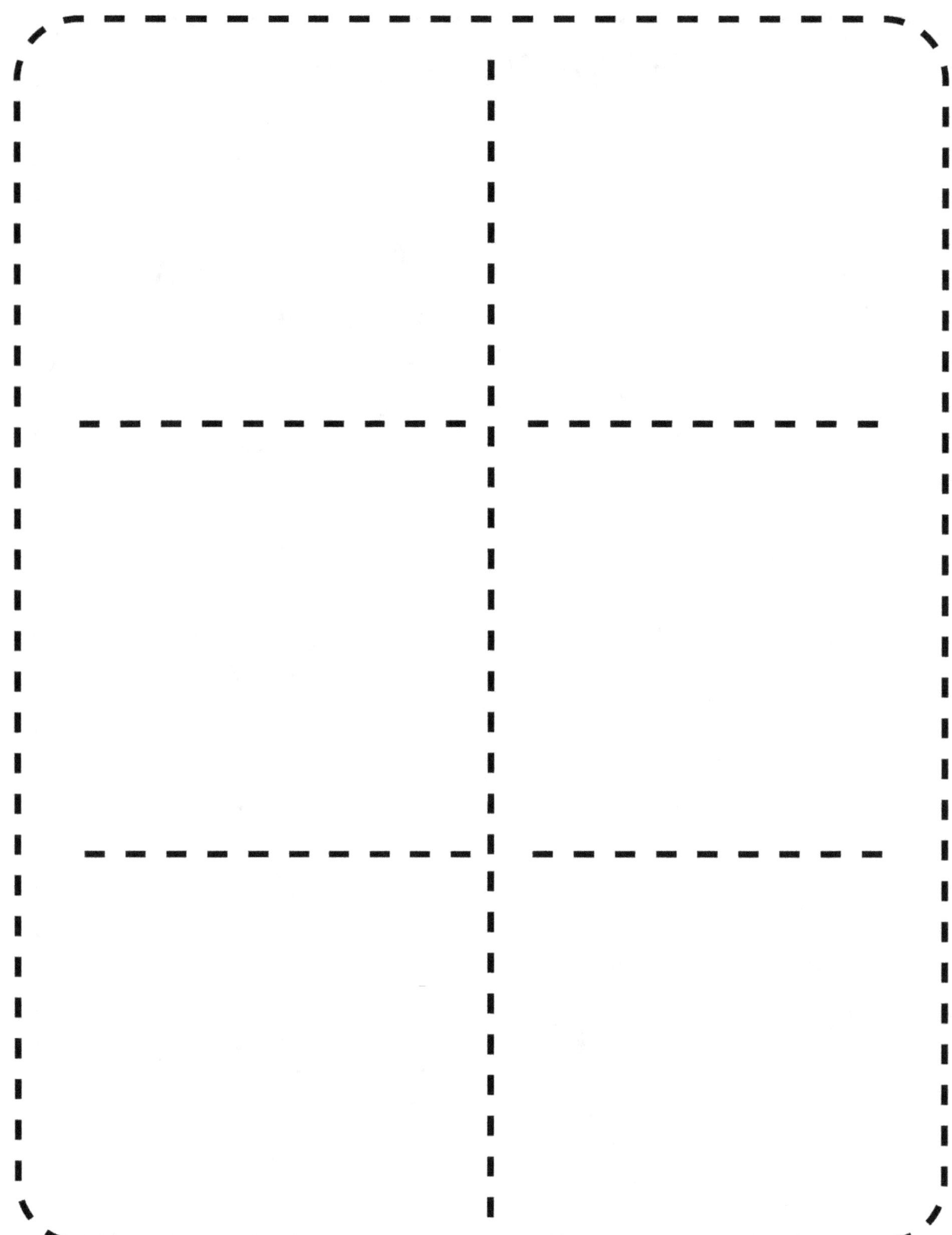

HOW TO DRAW

STEP 1

STEP 2

STEP 3

STEP 4

STEP 5

STEP 6

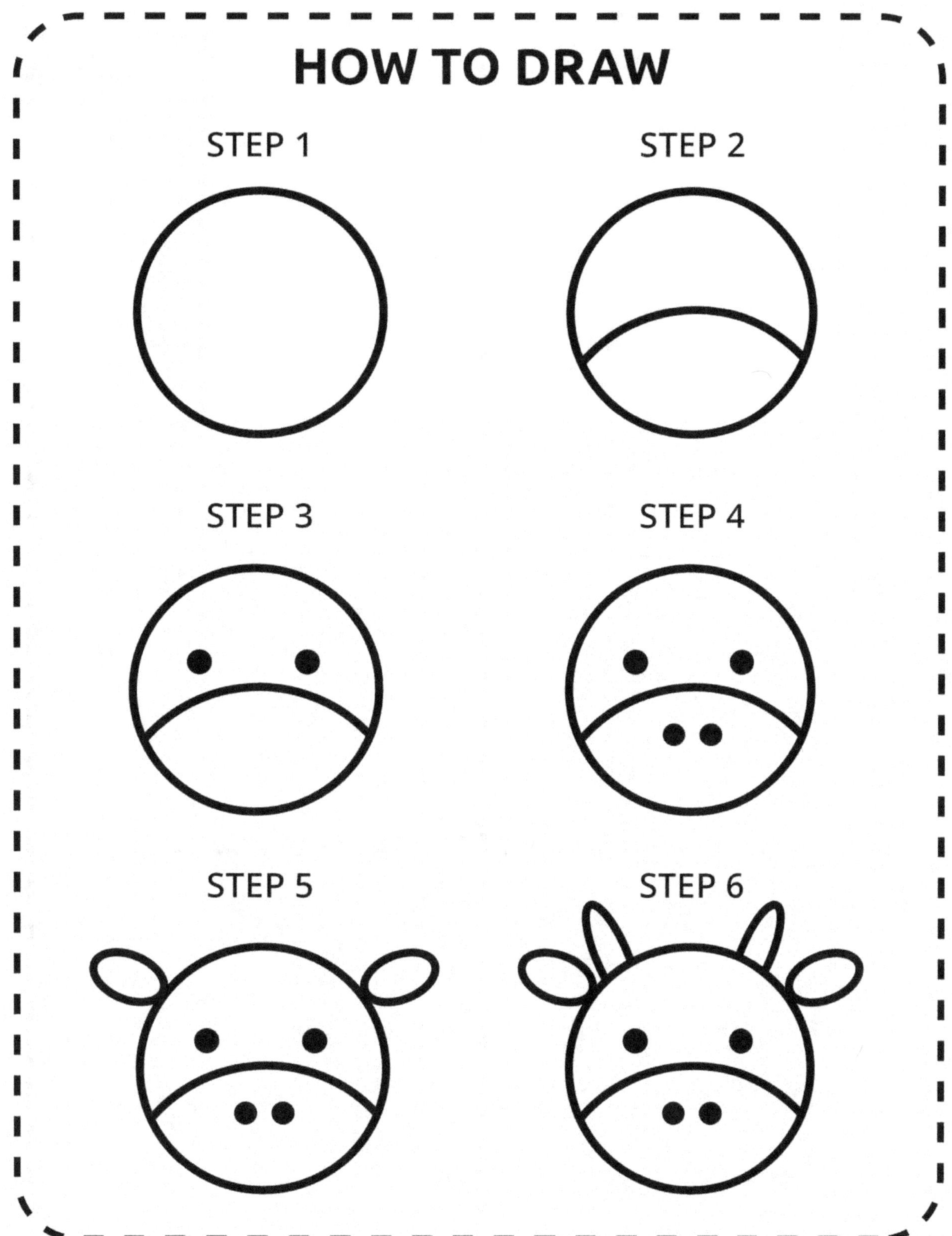

HOW TO DRAW

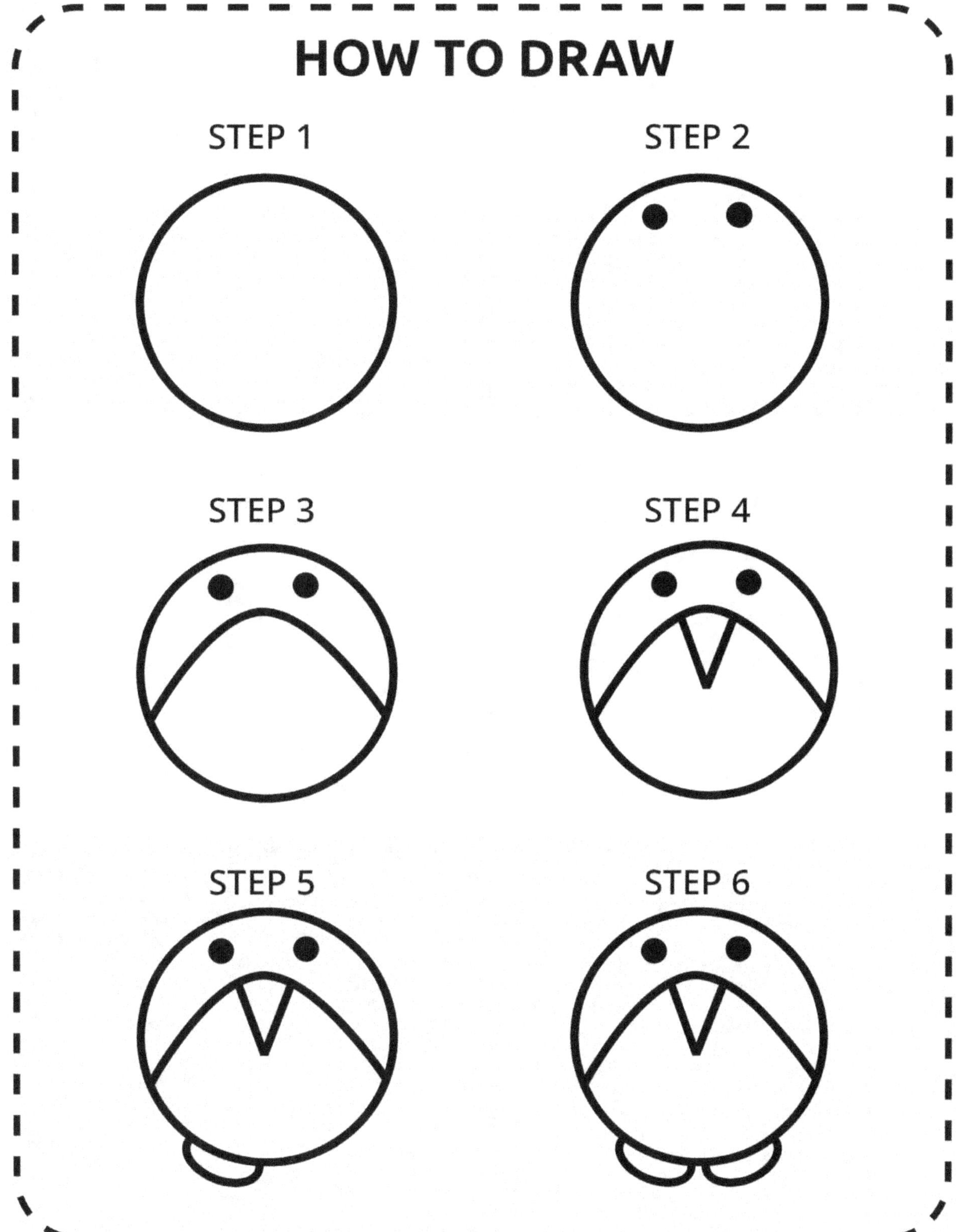

HOW TO DRAW

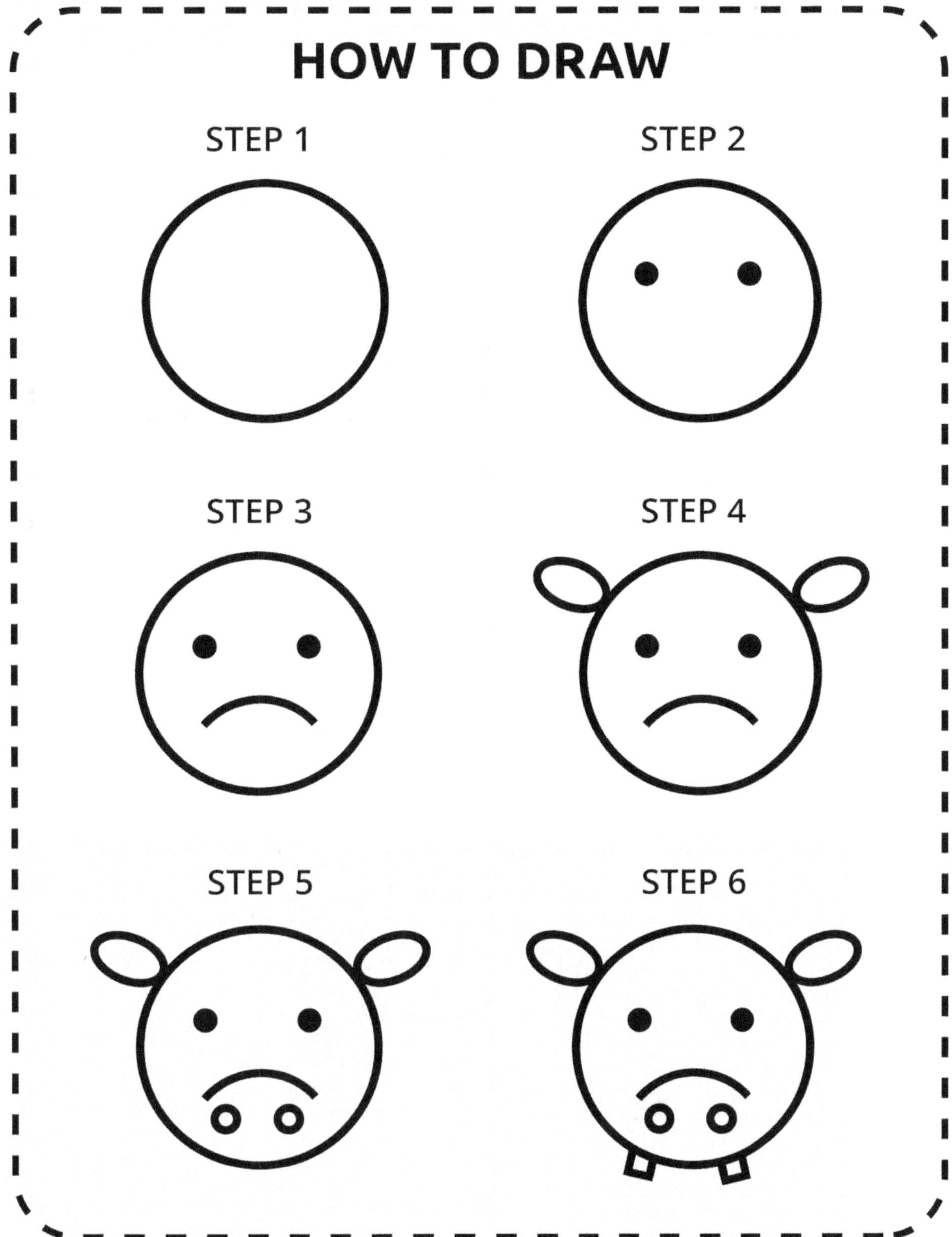

HOW TO DRAW

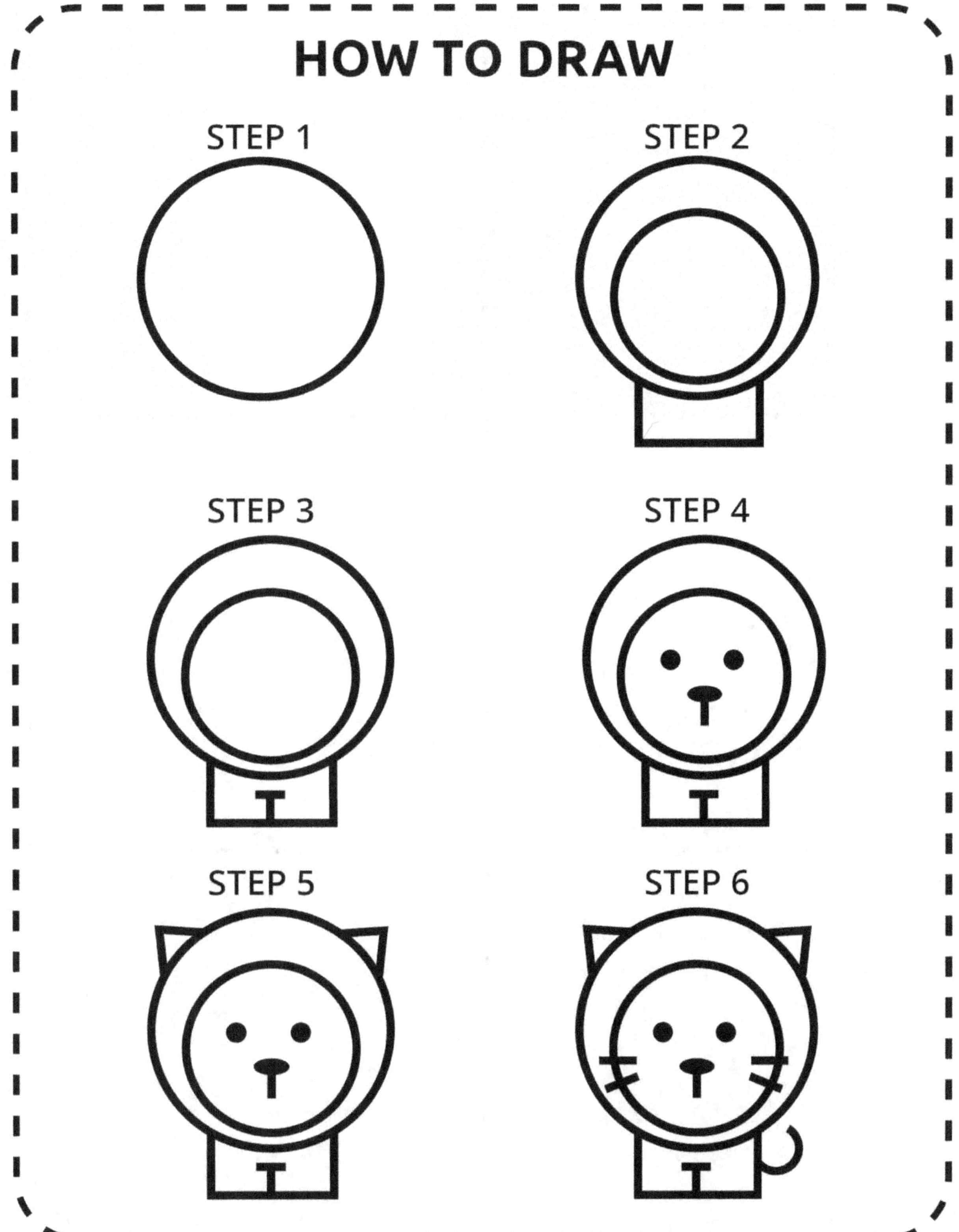

HOW TO DRAW

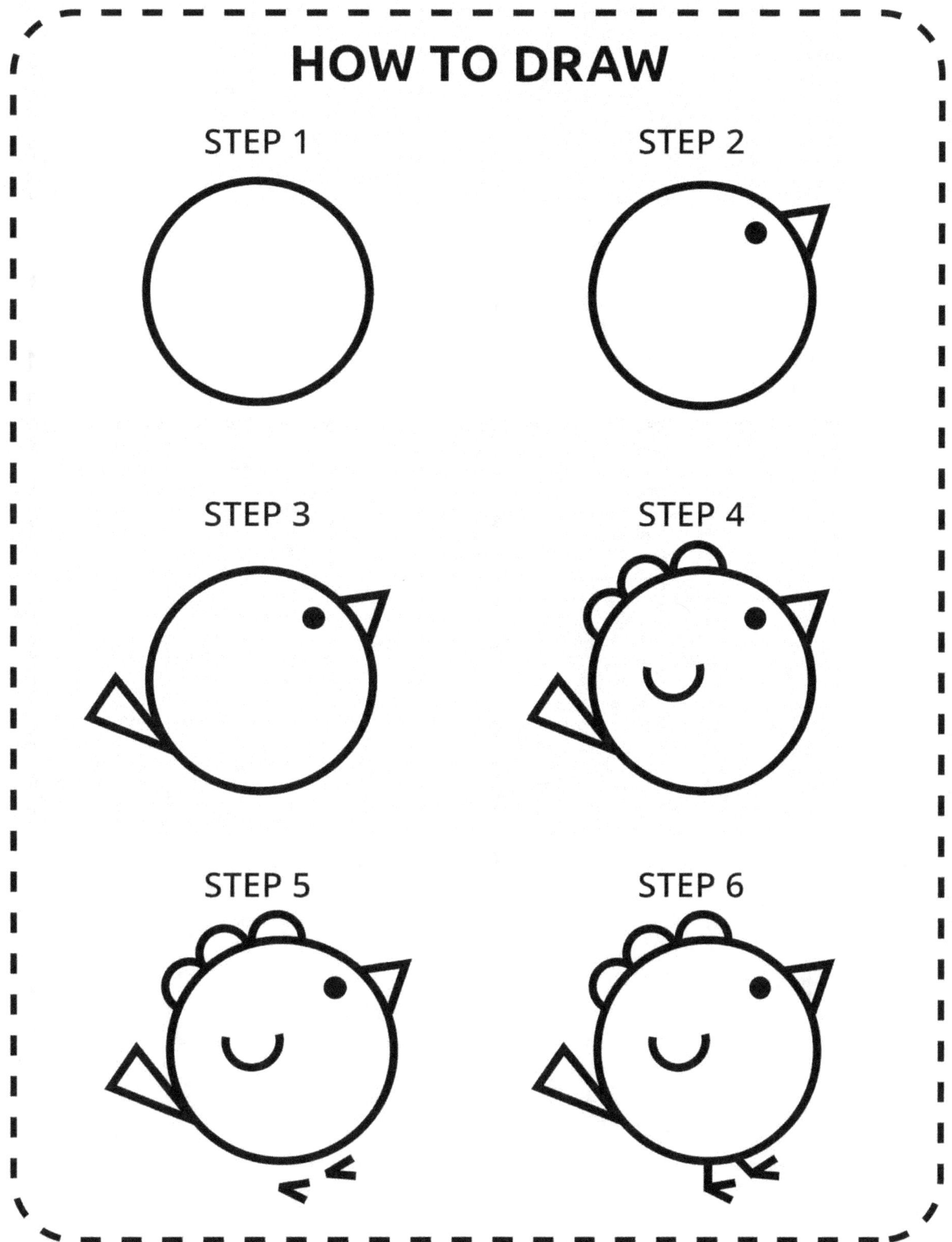

HOW TO DRAW

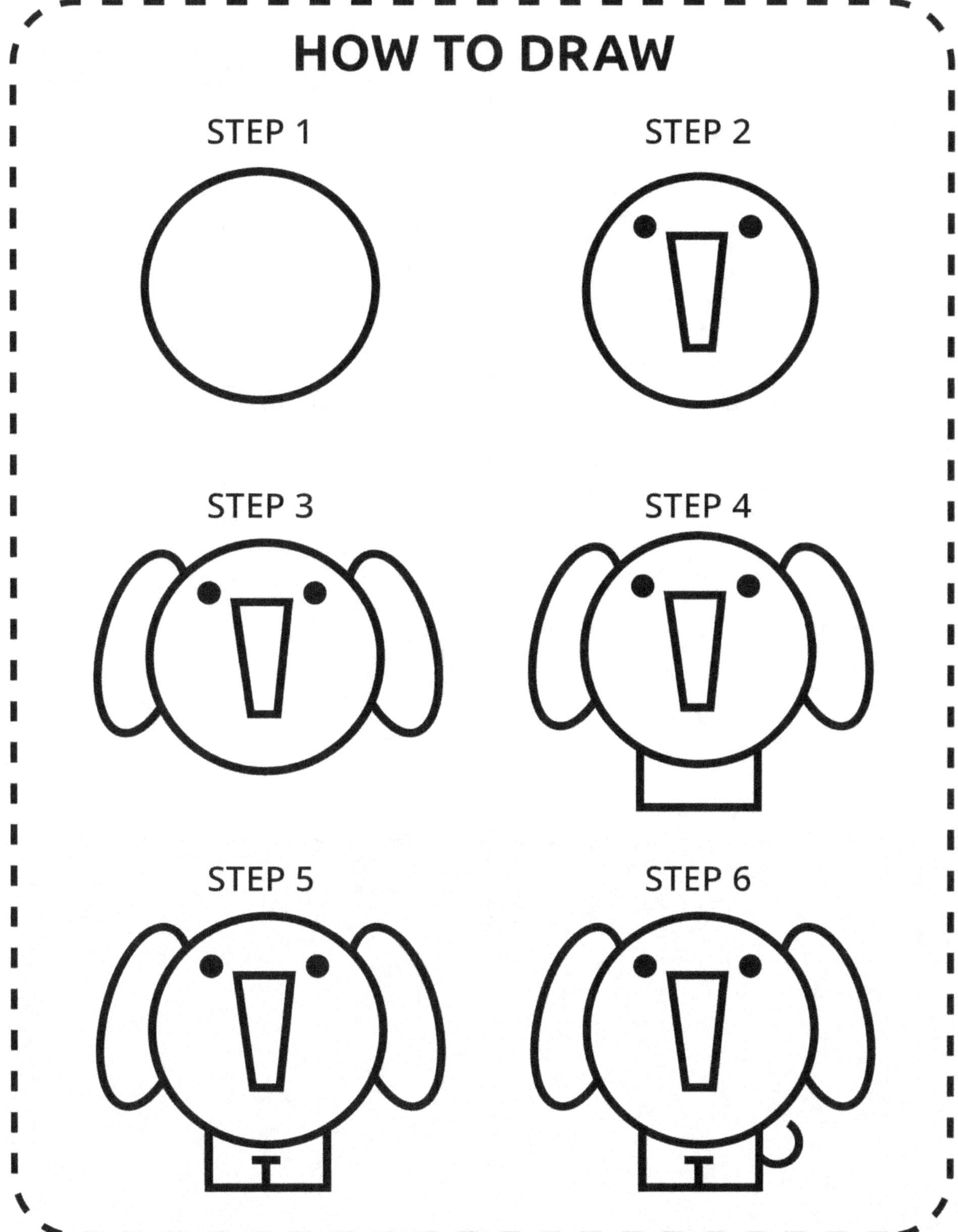

HOW TO DRAW

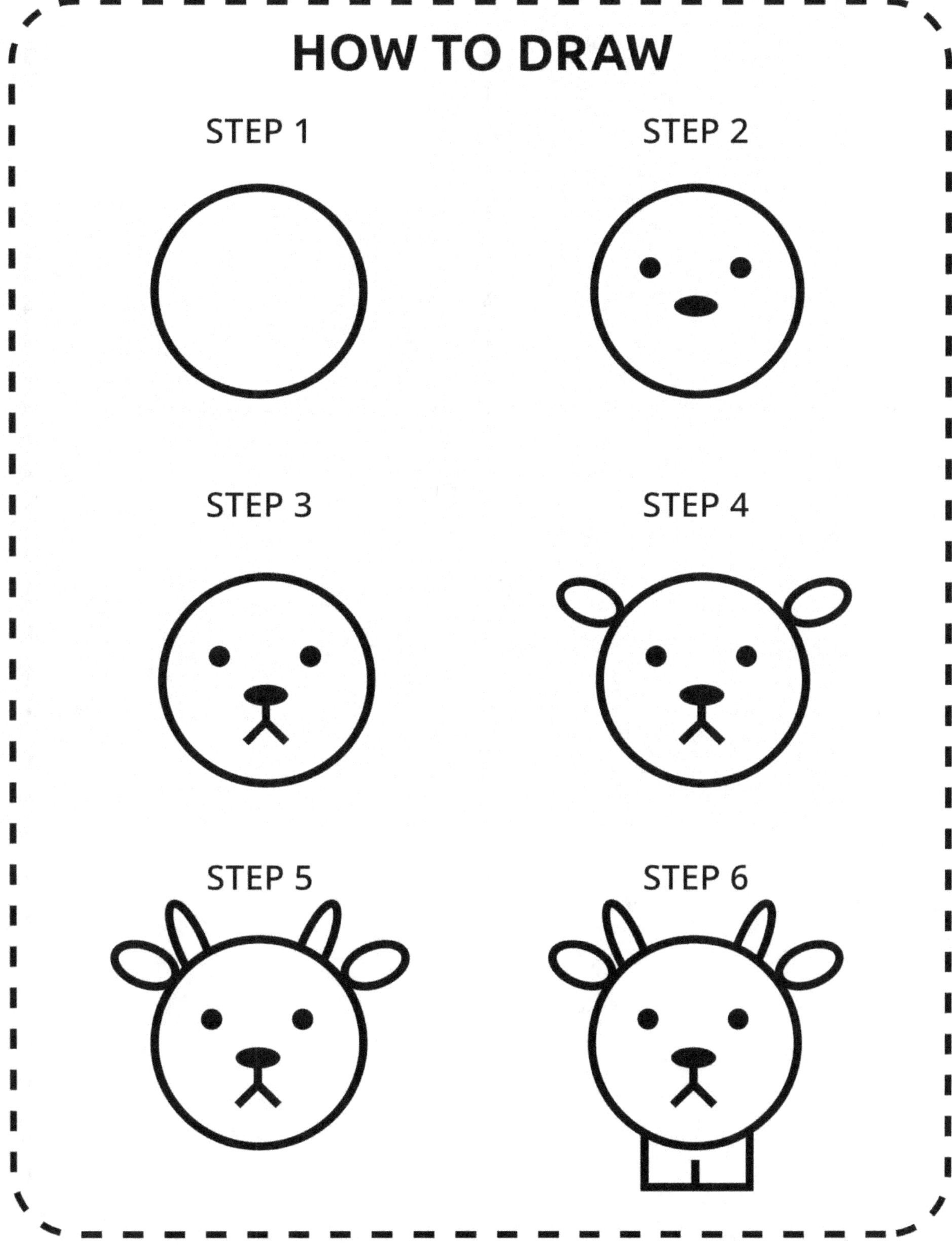

HOW TO DRAW

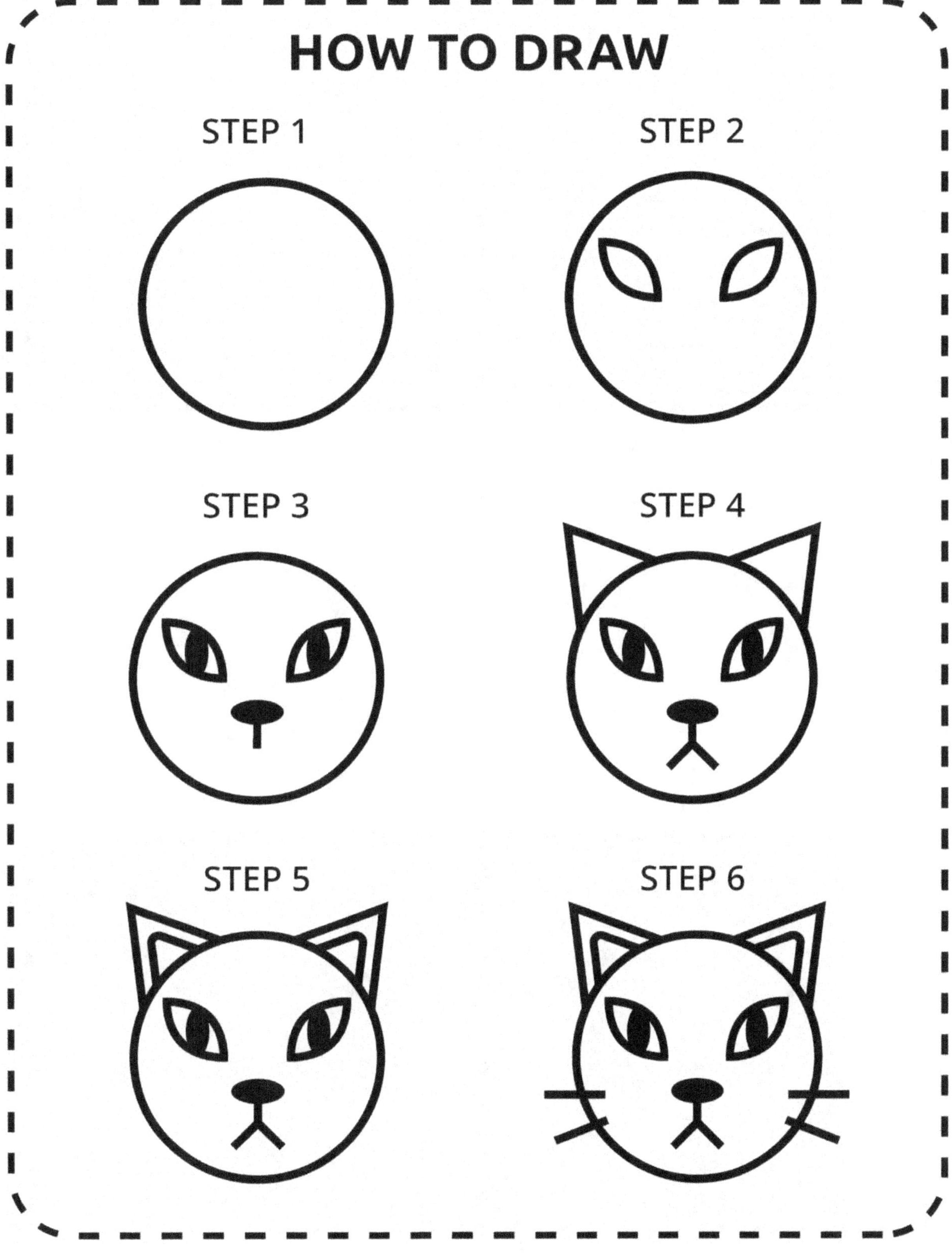

HOW TO DRAW

STEP 1

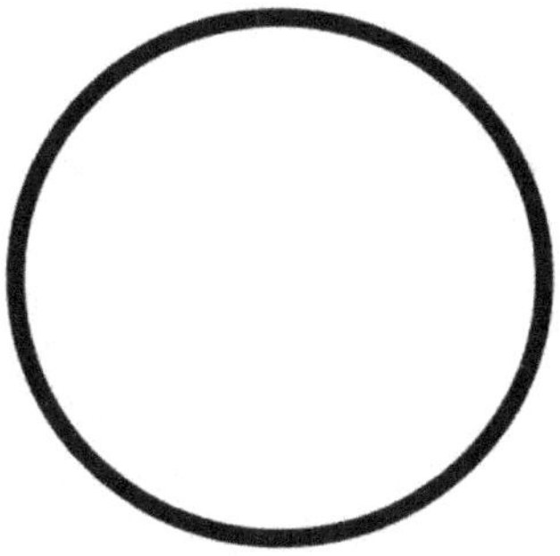

STEP 2

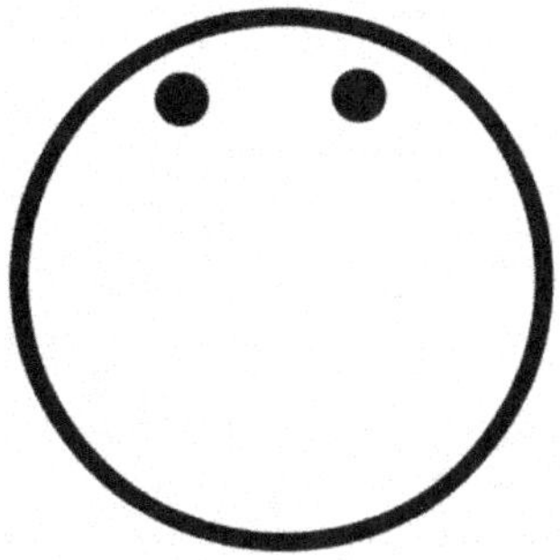

STEP 3

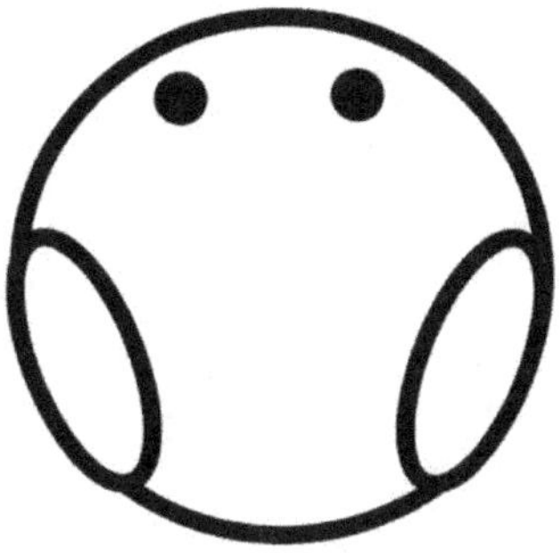

STEP 4

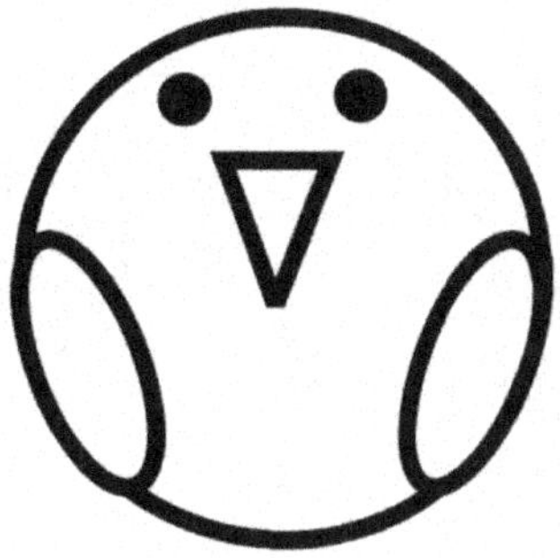

STEP 5

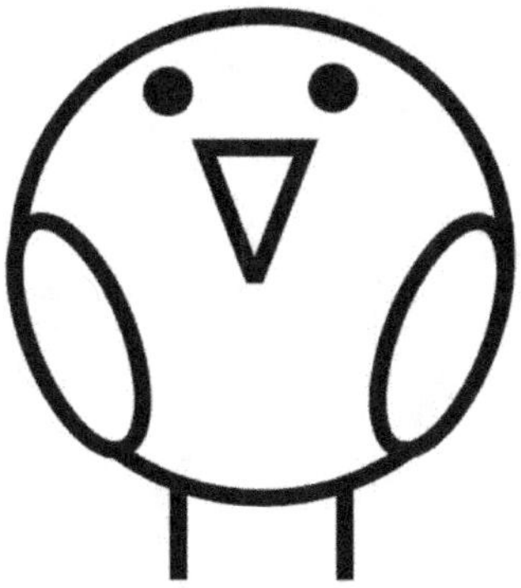

STEP 6

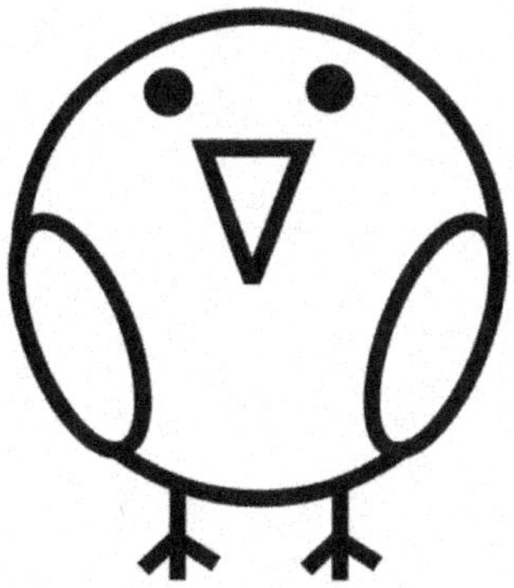

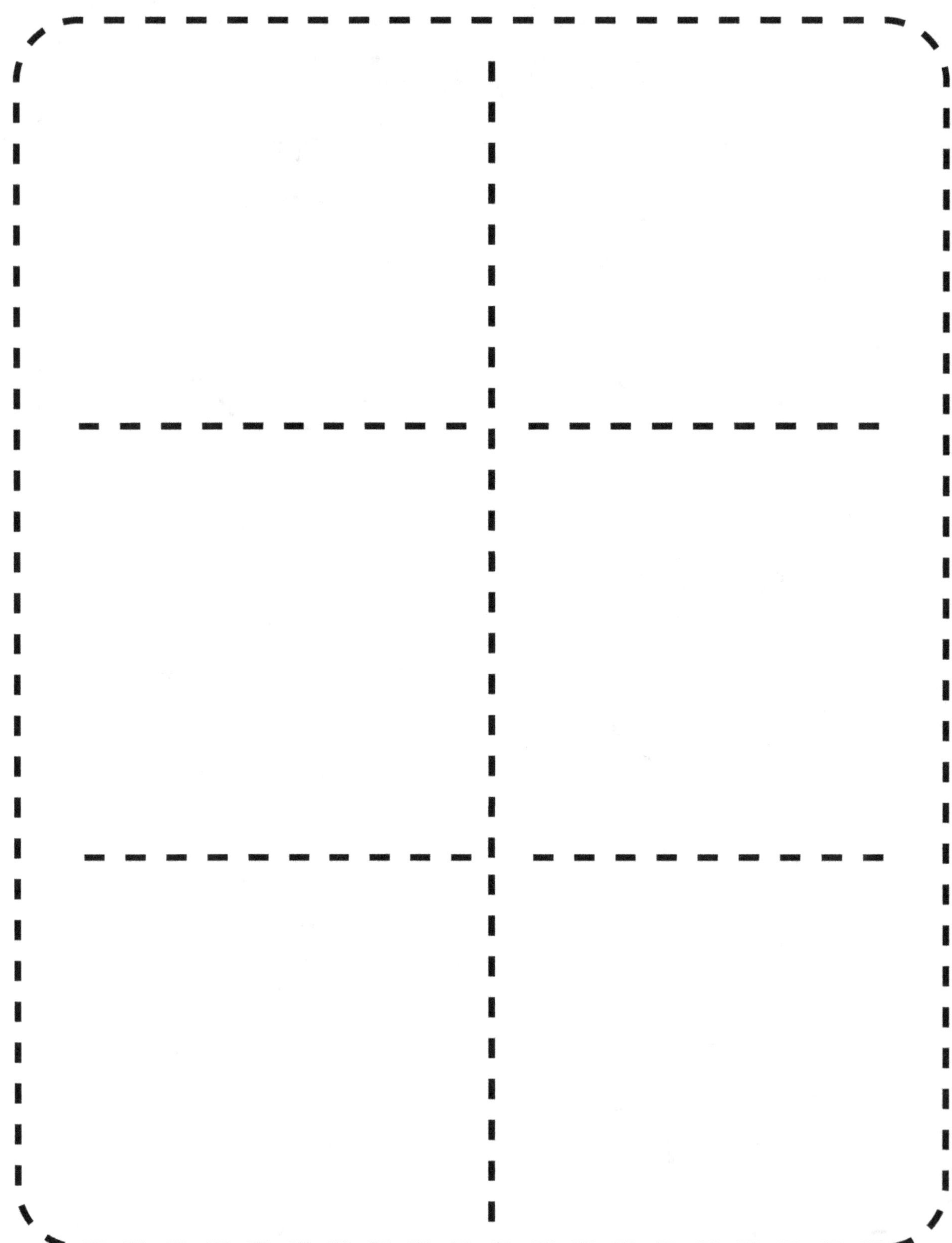

HOW TO DRAW

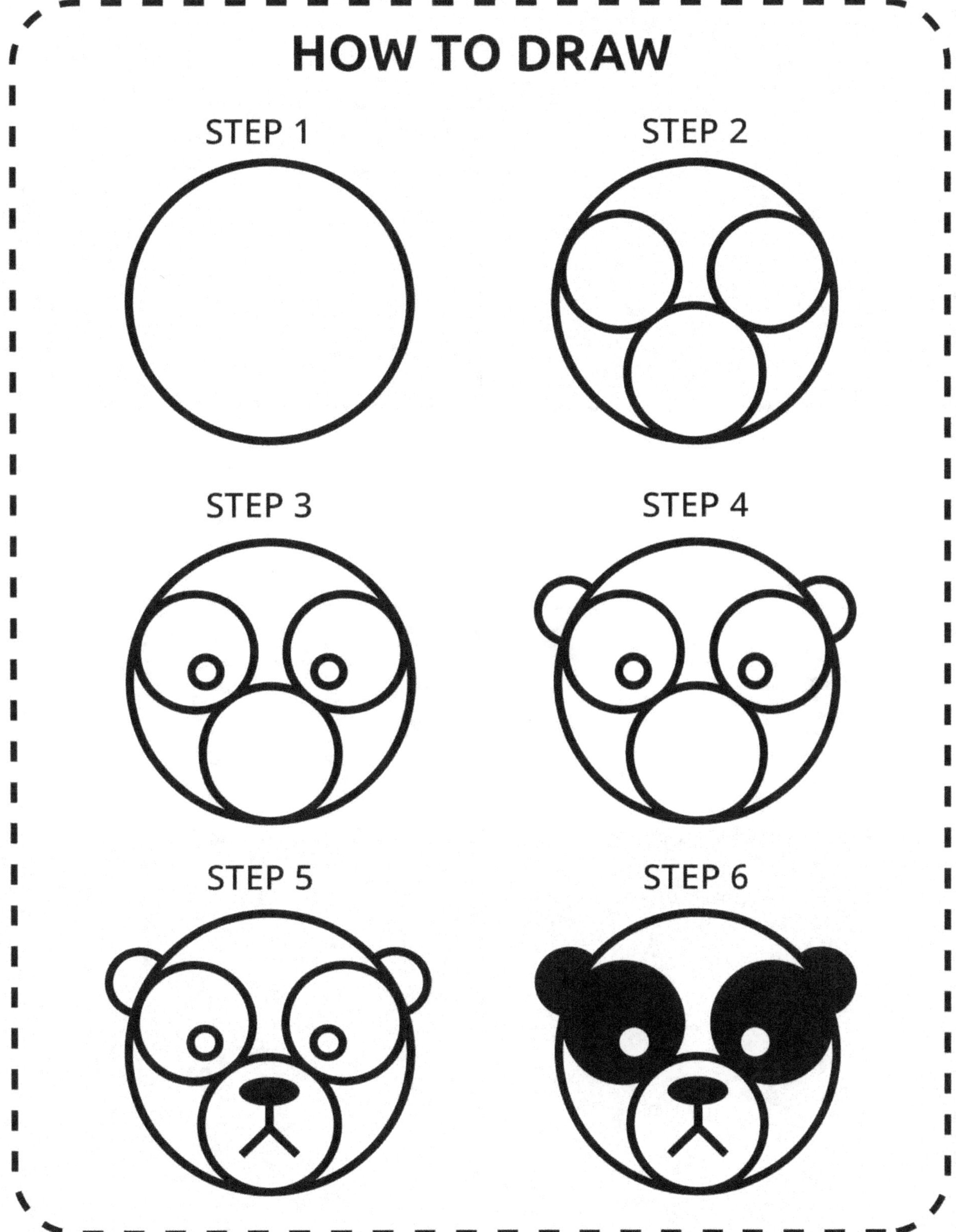

HOW TO DRAW

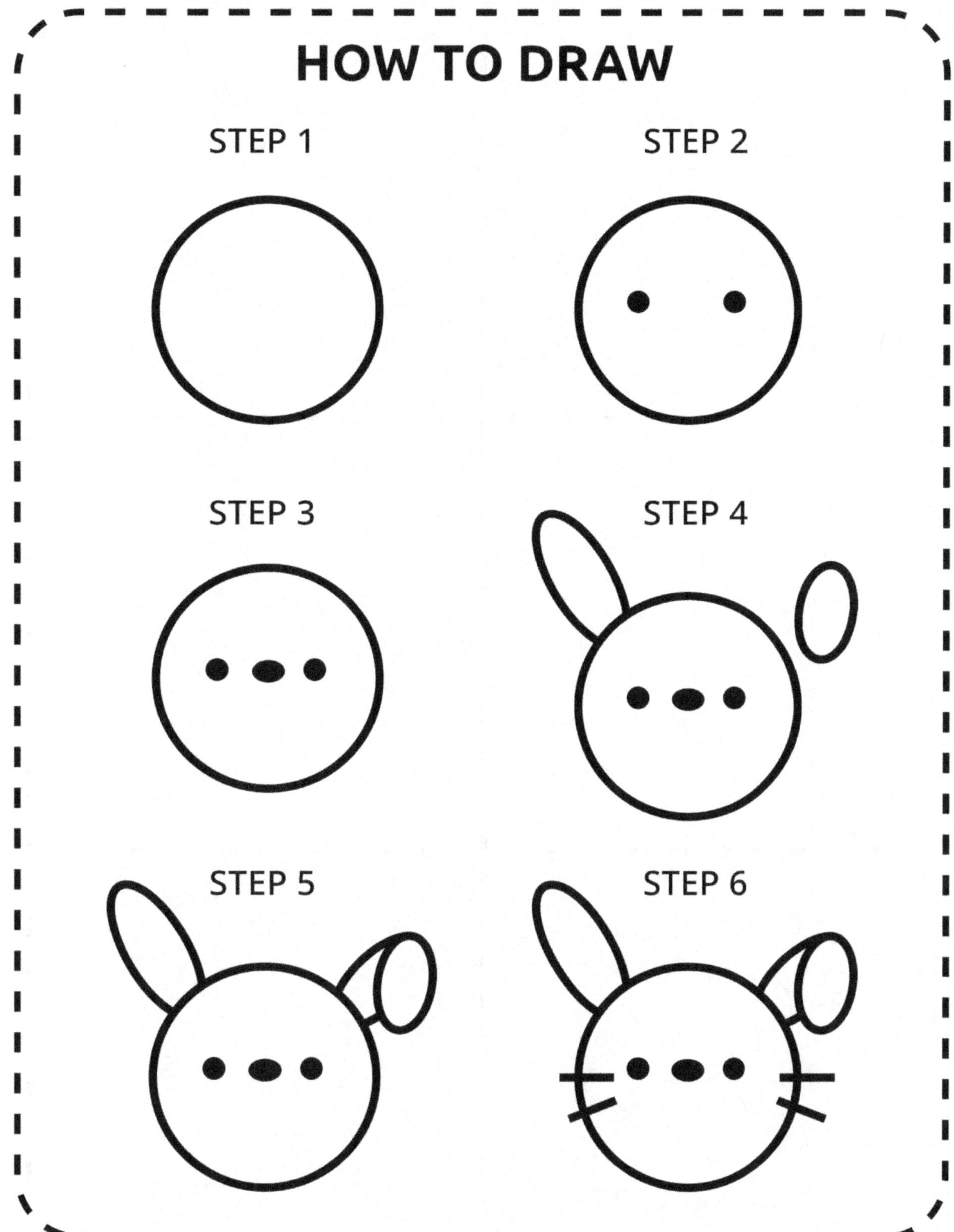

HOW TO DRAW

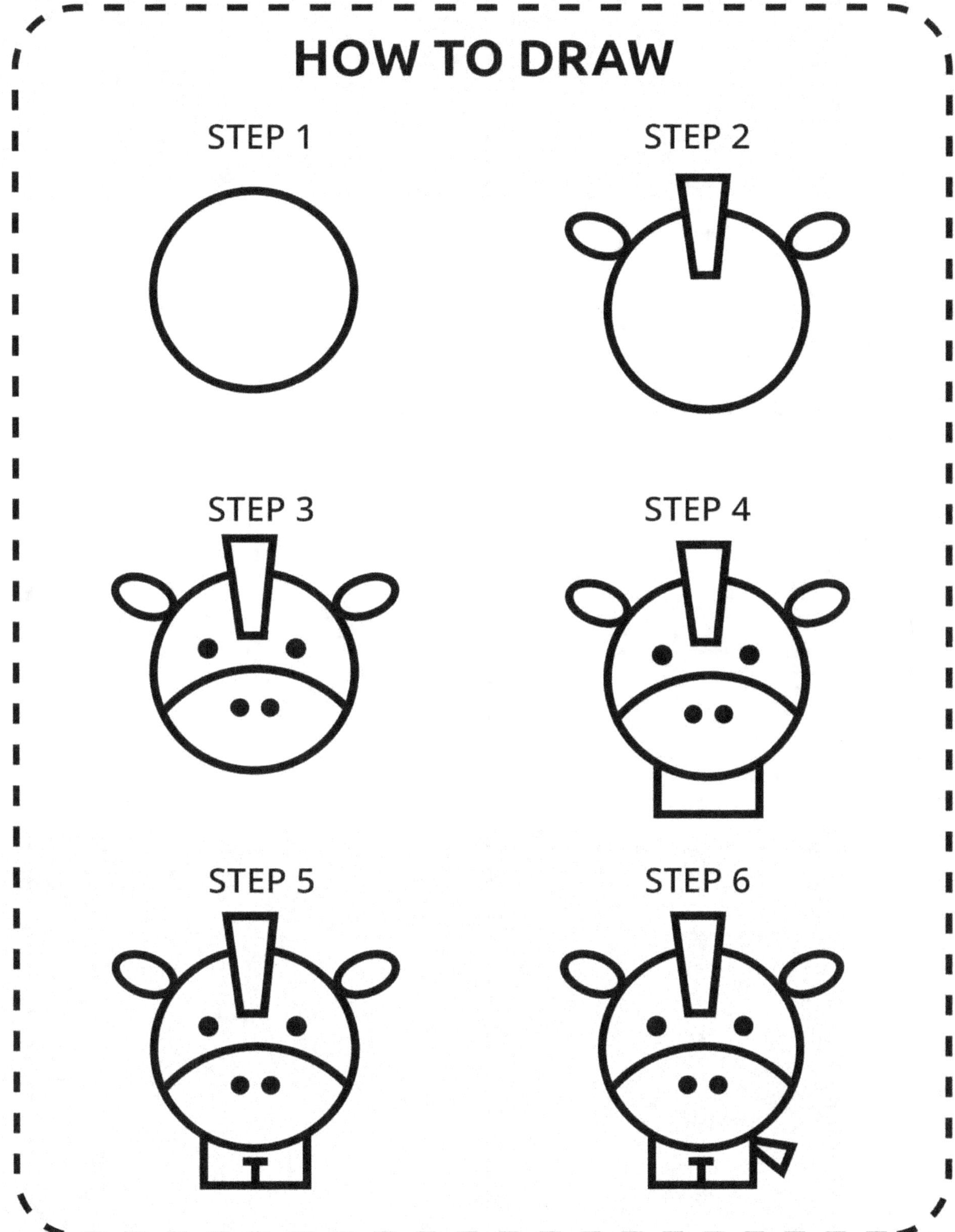

HOW TO DRAW

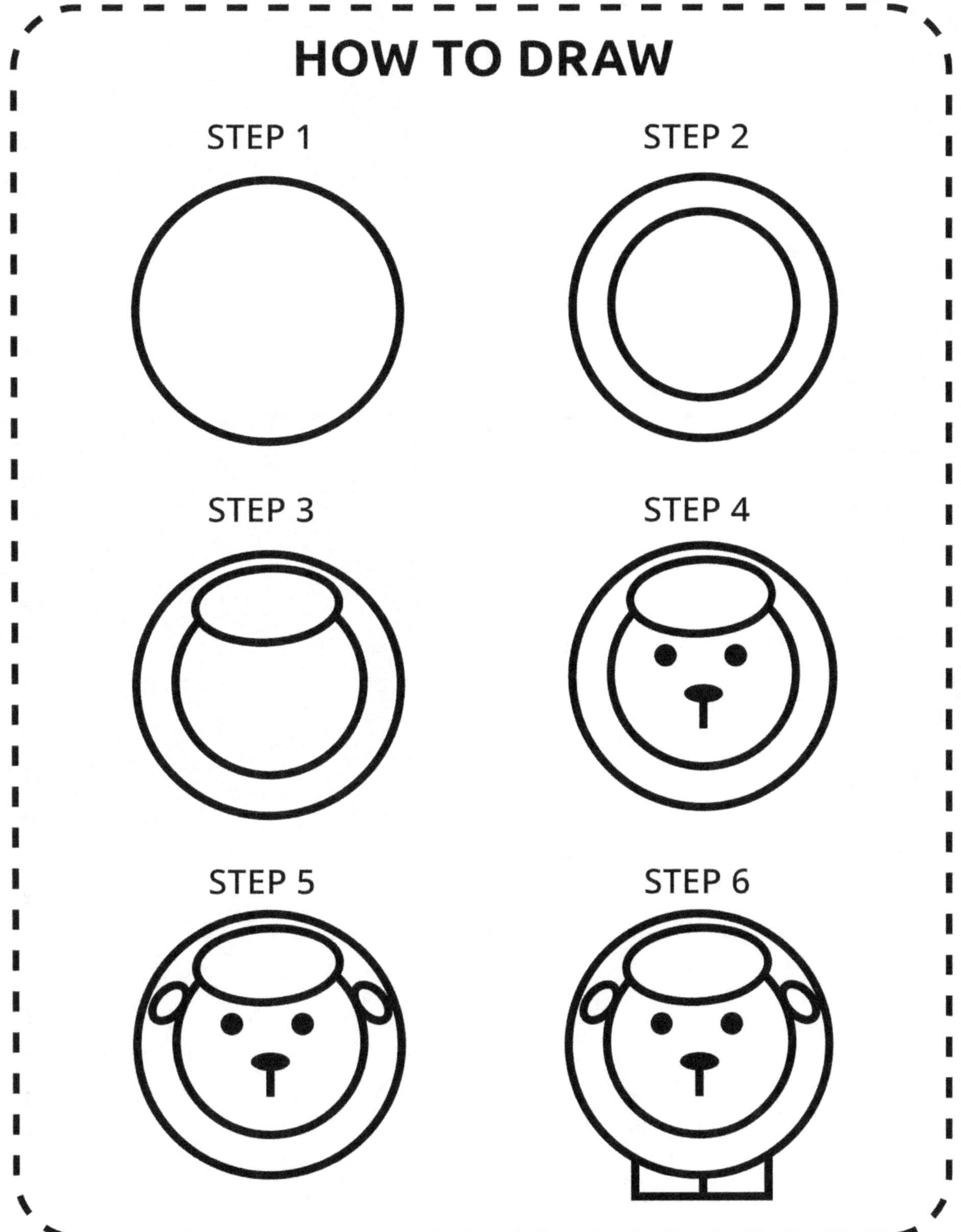

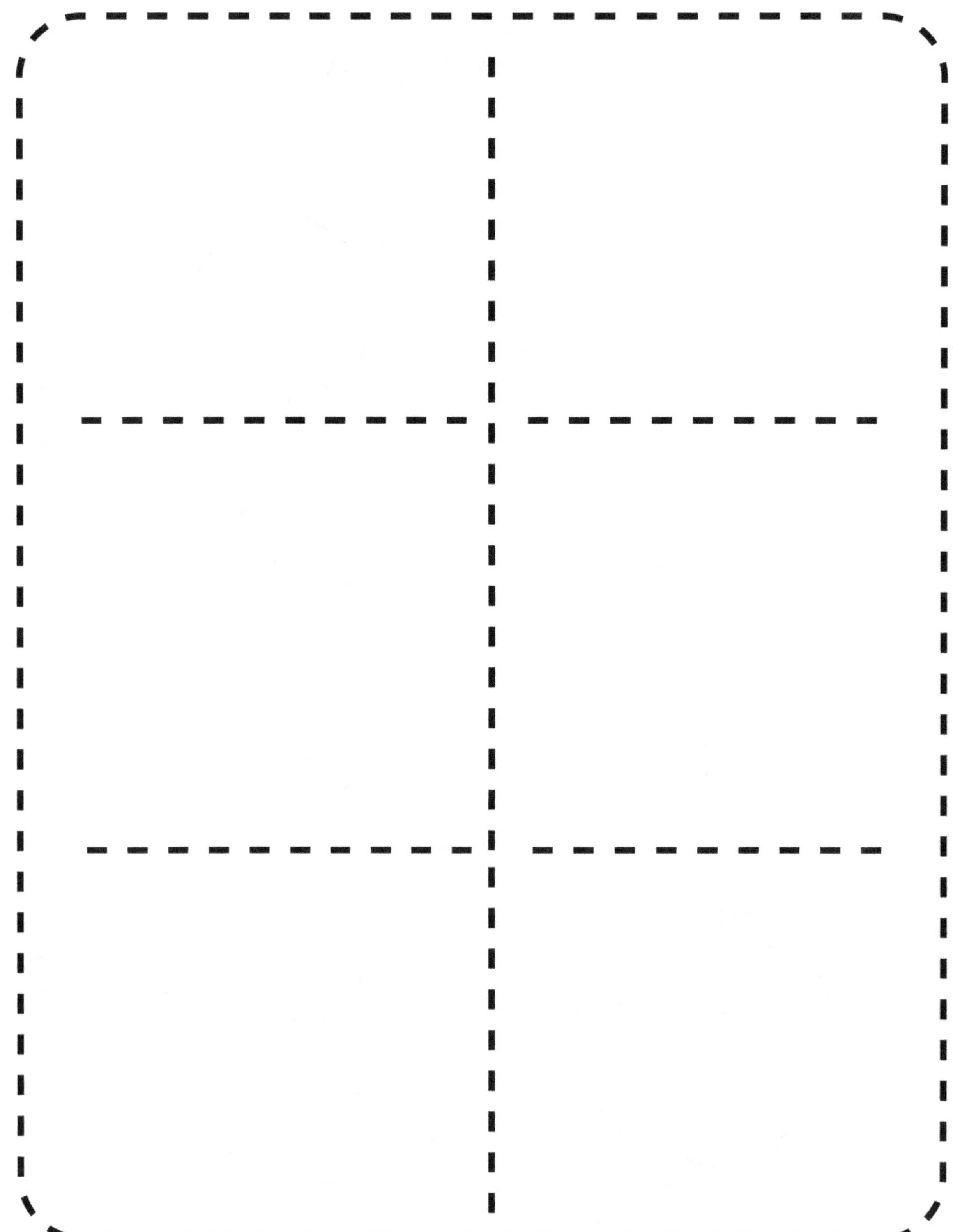

HOW TO DRAW

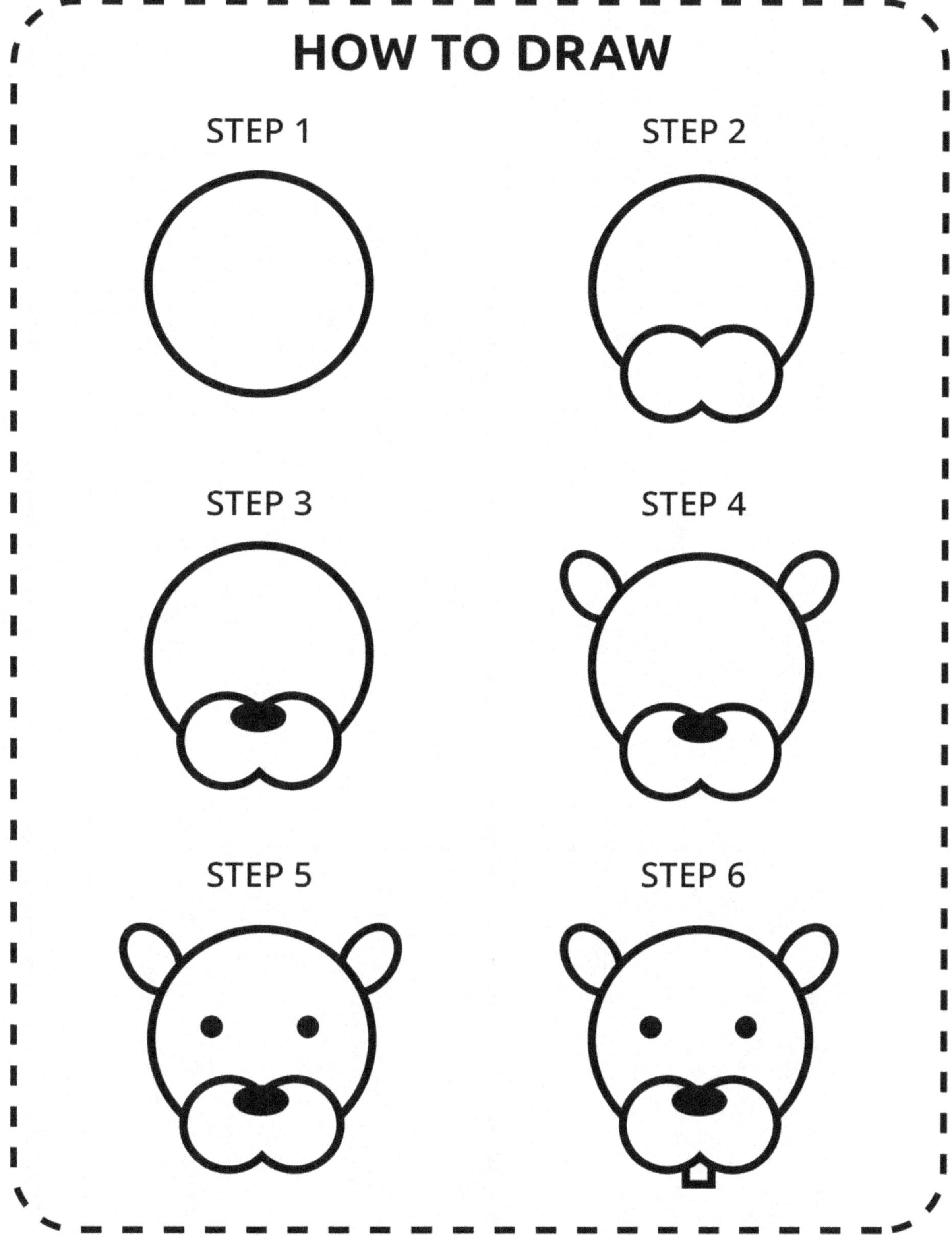

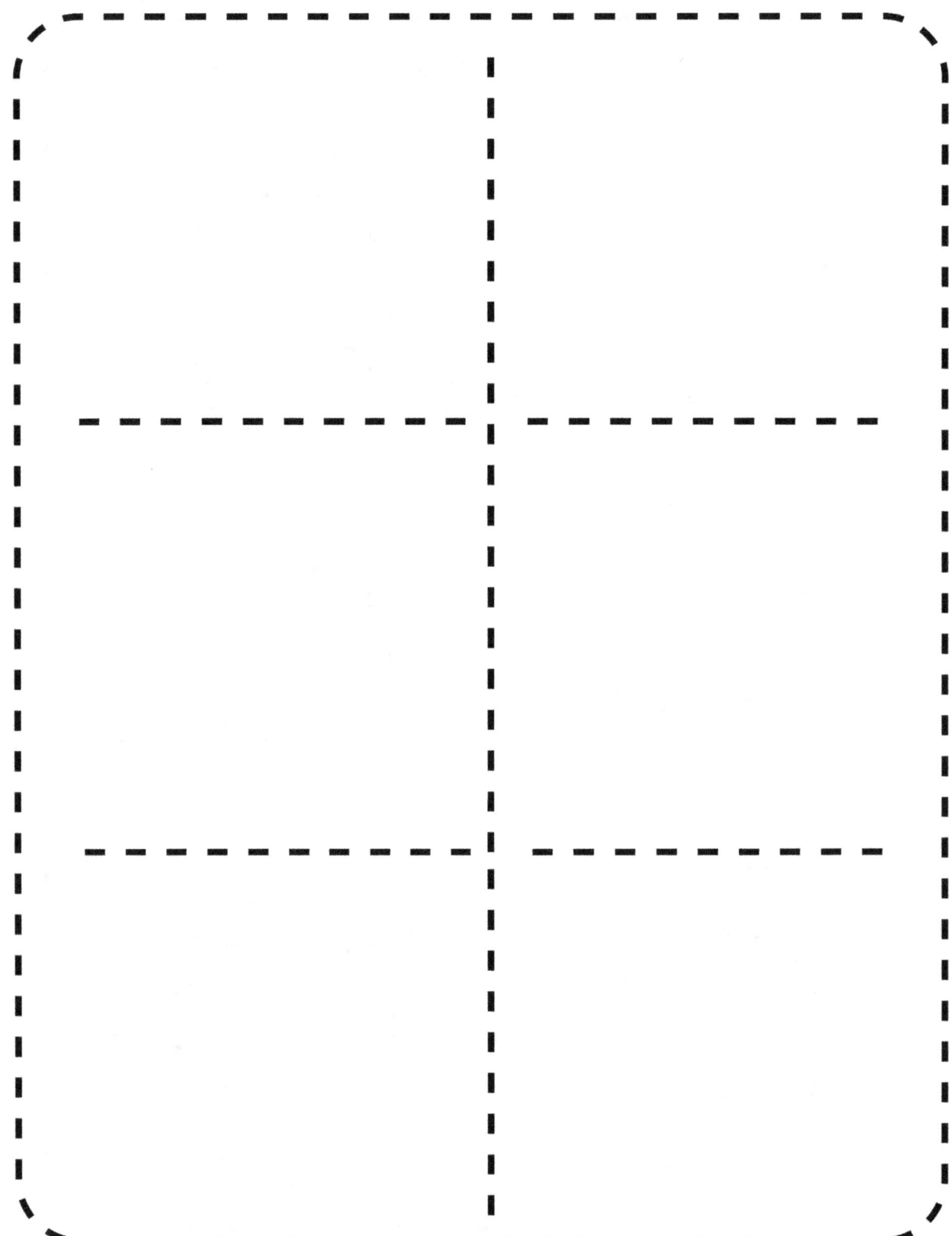

HOW TO DRAW

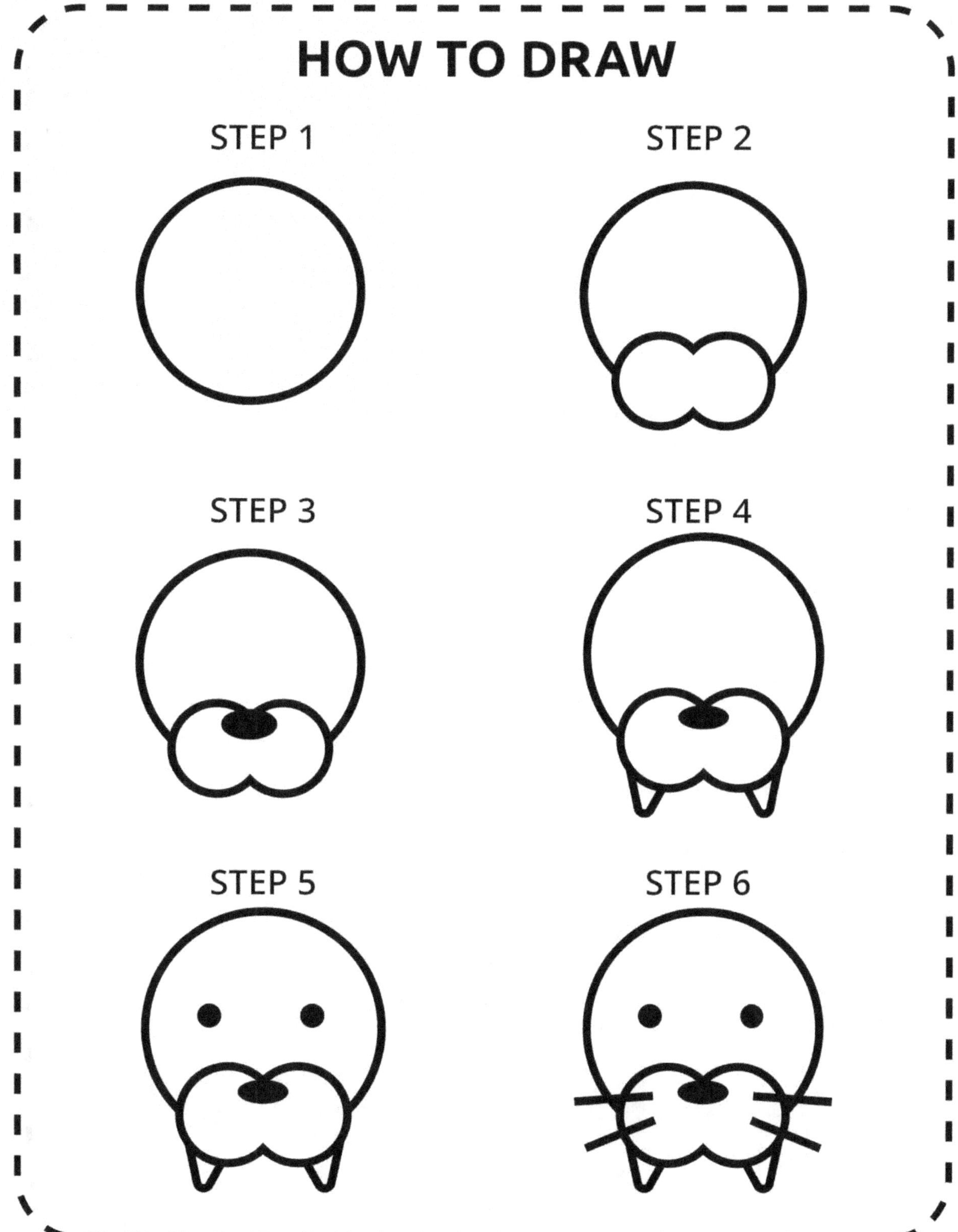

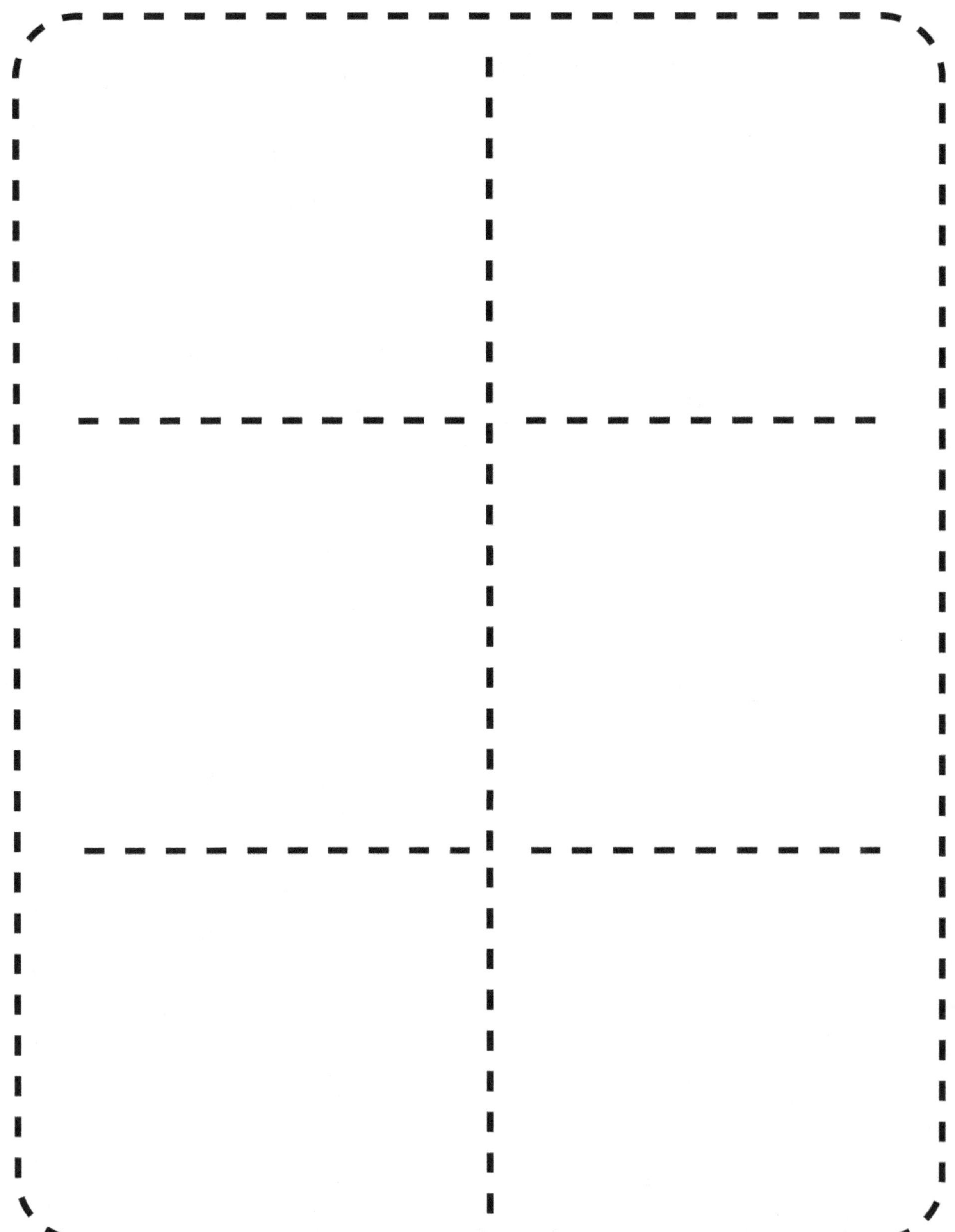

HOW TO DRAW

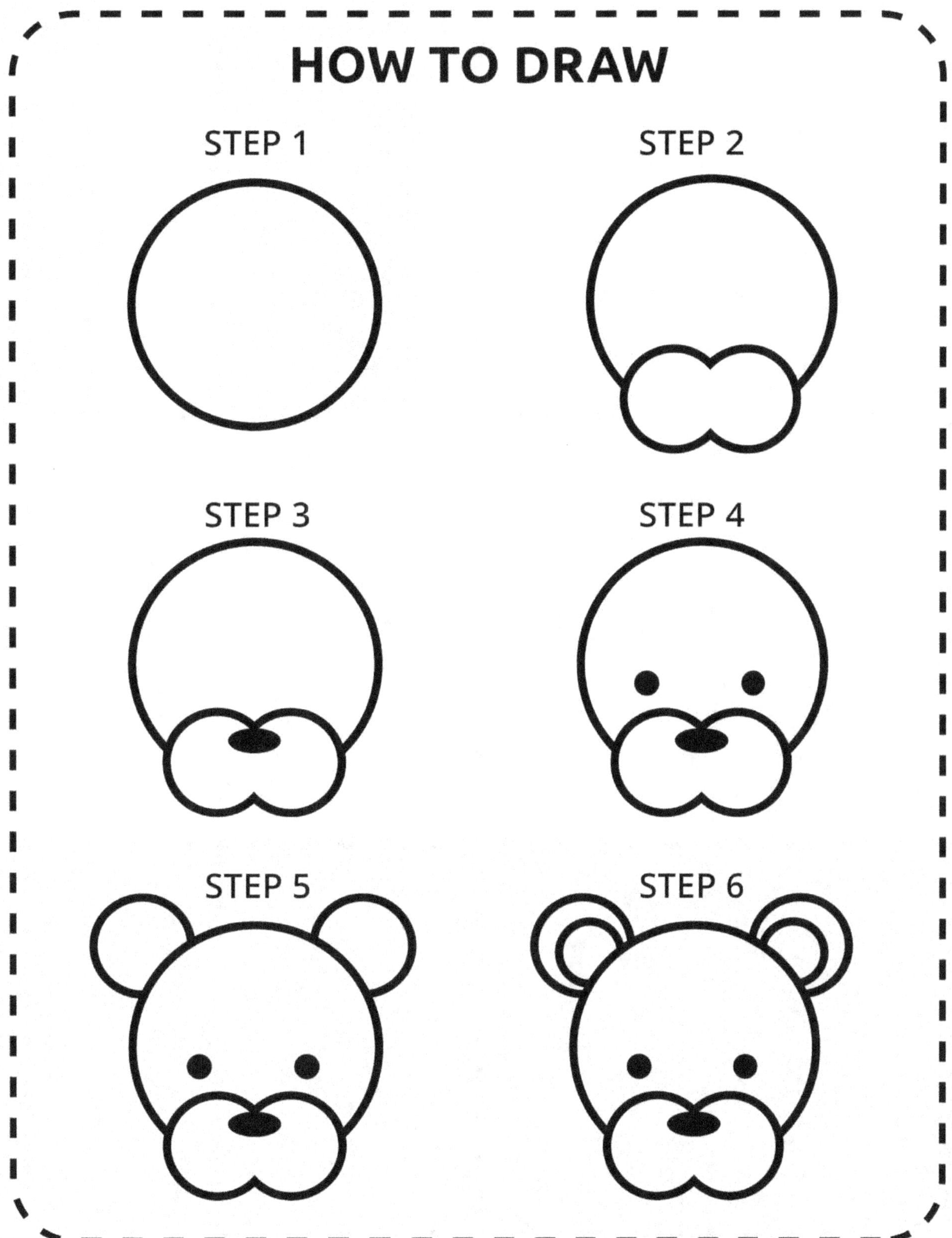

HOW TO DRAW

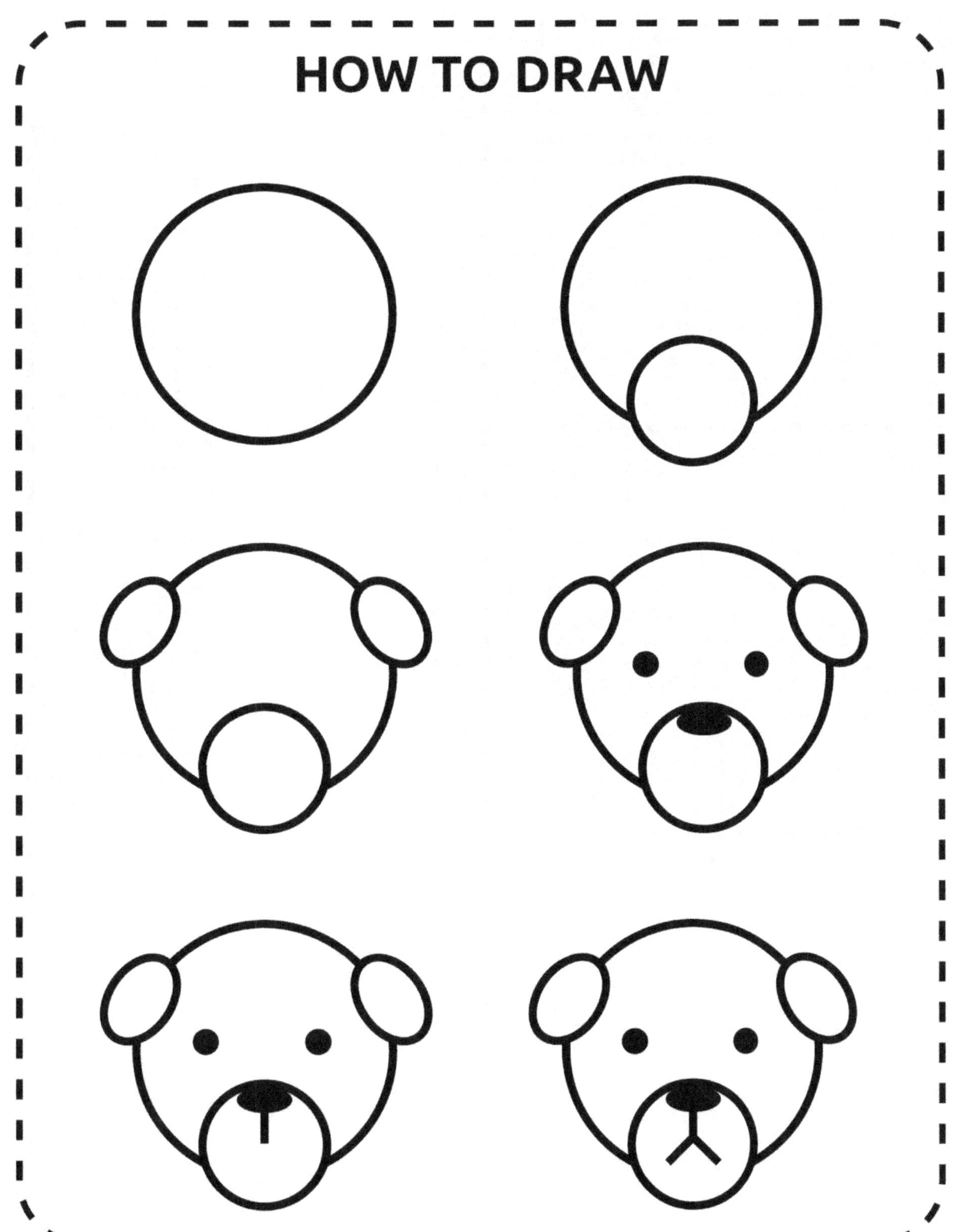

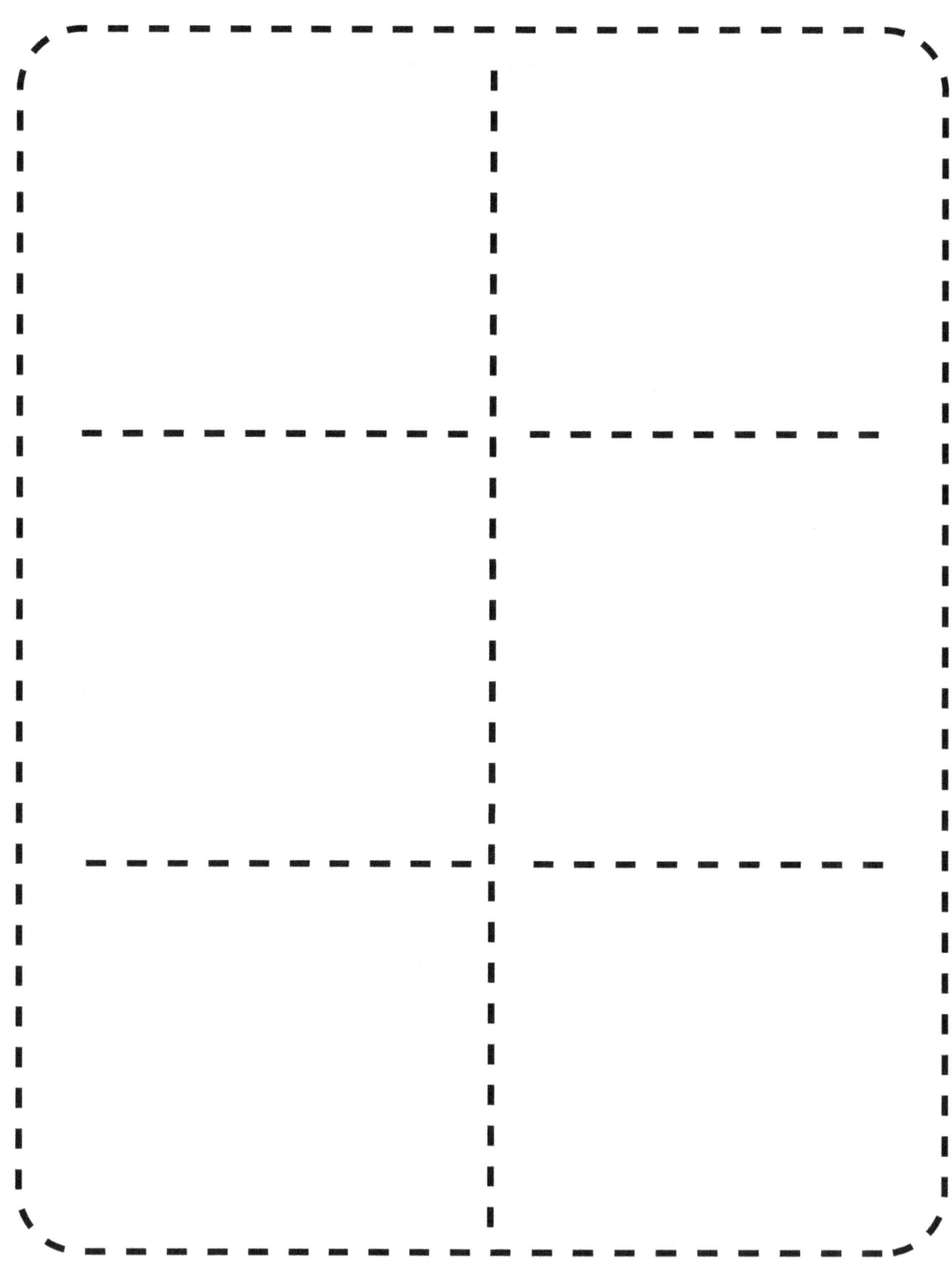

THANKS FOR YOUR PURCHASE